This book is dedicated to
all those fortunate people whose lives
were enriched and illuminated
by the golden days of the cinema.

Contents

		Page
	FOREWORD	4
I	DOVER	5
II	DEAL and WALMER	54
III	FOLKESTONE	73
IV	FOLKESTONE IN WARTIME, 1939-1945	108
	ACKNOWLEDGEMENTS	166

Foreword

When we decided to appeal through the local press and radio for information about the cinemas of Dover, Deal and Folkestone, the response was as though a dam had burst. Flooding towards us came a torrent of affectionate memories and anecdotes, together with photos, programmes, newspaper cuttings and good wishes. Many letters and telephone calls came from folk who had worked in cinemas in peace and war: managers, projectionists and usherettes. But the bulk came from filmgoers who, like us, were entertained and educated (in the widest sense) by the most wonderful window-on-the-world that had so far been invented.

But why did we pick on the cinemas of Dover, Deal and Folkestone? First, because we have spent many happy hours in at least some of the cinemas in the three towns, but more importantly because in our view the role of the cinema in time of war in providing comfort and cheer to all those in H.M. Forces and civilians, has never been widely appreciated, so that the "Hellfire Corner" cinemas provide a unique sample of entertainment centres which helped to win World War II by boosting morale.

Our book, therefore, sets out to give the histories of the cinemas of the three towns, spanning peace and war, with one chapter wholly devoted to the cinemas of Folkestone during World War II. Although we provide many facts and figures, the whole is illuminated we hope, by illustrations and quotations which will enable readers to re-live the days when a visit to The Pictures was a way of life.

THE AUTHORS

B.F.I.

INTO THE ABYSS. The White Cliffs town of DOVER has no public cinemas now. DEAL has the tiny FLICKS cinema which has survived the conversion of the CLASSIC (ex ODEON) into an amusement arcade and pool hall. FOLKESTONE has the triple-screen CANNON (ex CLASSIC). Nationally, of the 5500 cinemas open in 1939, about 700 remain with some 1200 screens, allowing for the twinned and tripled cinemas. Audiences in 1946 were 31 million a week, but by 1982 had slumped to 1.5 million a week. In the year 1984 just 64 million admissions were recorded. The admissions figure for 1986 was 72.6 million, an increase of 3.5% on 1985.

PICTURE PALACES REMEMBERED

An affectionate look at the
Cinema Theatres
of
Dover, Deal and Folkestone

by
John Roy
&
Tony Thompson

GLENTON PUBLICATIONS
68 Valley Road, River, Dover, Kent CT17 0QW

First published in 1987 by GLENTON PUBLICATIONS.

© JOHN ROY and TONY THOMPSON, 1987.

ISBN 0 9512825 0 6

All rights reserved. No part of this publication may be reproduced, stored in a retrieval system, or transmitted, in any form or by any means, electronic, mechanical, photocopying, recording or otherwise without the prior permission of the publishers. Such permission, if granted, may be subject to fee depending on the nature of the use.

The profits from the sale of this book will be donated to the **EAST KENT HOSPICE**

Designed & Printed in Great Britain by
A.R. Adams & Sons (Printers) Ltd,
Dover, Kent CT16 1PY.

PART ONE

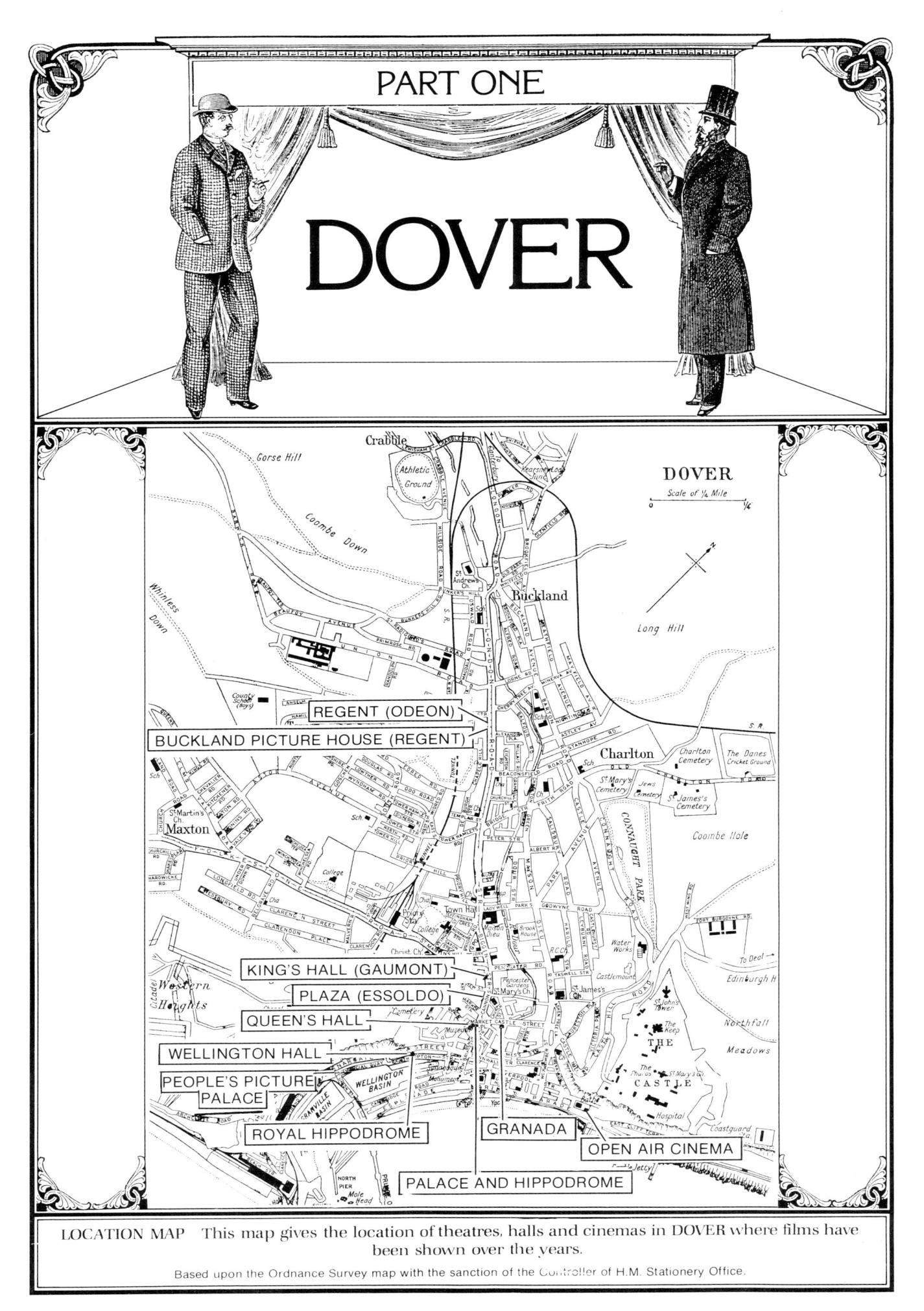

DOVER

DOVER
Scale of ¼ Mile

- REGENT (ODEON)
- BUCKLAND PICTURE HOUSE (REGENT)
- KING'S HALL (GAUMONT)
- PLAZA (ESSOLDO)
- QUEEN'S HALL
- WELLINGTON HALL
- PEOPLE'S PICTURE PALACE
- ROYAL HIPPODROME
- GRANADA
- OPEN AIR CINEMA
- PALACE AND HIPPODROME

LOCATION MAP   This map gives the location of theatres, halls and cinemas in DOVER where films have been shown over the years.
Based upon the Ordnance Survey map with the sanction of the Controller of H.M. Stationery Office.

Early Days

"The first Moving Picture Show which I saw in Dover was at a 'Showman's Stand' in an empty shop in Cannon Street when I was a small boy, say 1906-7. As far as I can recall, the picture ran for about ten minutes, was taken from the front of a mountain railway train, the only movement being that of passing countryside."
M.L. HOBDAY

The illustration shows a typical conversion of a shop front with the first floor window giving the public a clear view of the projection box. (From THE CINEMA TODAY by D.A. Spencer and H.D. Waley, pub. 1939 by Oxford University Press).

THE PALACE AND HIPPODROME, Market Square, originally the Empire Theatre of Varieties, claimed in December 1909 to be 'Dover's Original Picture Palace', boasting that 'We lead, others follow' and recommending prospective patrons to 'See all the other picture shows in Dover, then pay us a visit and see the best'. But a resident of The Gateway is on record as insisting that the first picture house in Dover was an upper room in the APOLLONIAN HOTEL, Snargate Street, advertised as the PEOPLE'S PICTURE PALACE. "You had to climb a wooden staircase and paid one penny to enter the picture house. I remember a woman thumping out a tune on the piano, while a man pointed out the words to the song with a black stick; we used to sing our heads off." THE PALACE AND HIPPODROME stood empty for years, but was opened as an occupational centre for the unemployed of Dover in 1933; subsequently it was demolished.

THE ROYAL HIPPODROME, Snargate Street, an historic playhouse dating back to 1790, regularly included 'Hippodrome Pictures' in its programmes, an added attraction to the variety turns which justified the title 'The Premier Theatre of Varieties in Dover'. On 18 September, 1944, a 16" German shell hit the theatre, putting it out of business. Demolition took place in 1951, the site being used to build a timber yard.

THE TOWN HALL and PIER PAVILION. There were occasional showings of cinematograph pictures at these venues, the Town Council granting licences as and when required. The pier and its Pavilion were demolished in 1927.

THE QUEEN'S HALL, Queen Street, was undoubtedly Dover's first real picture house, albeit a converted property, opening its doors on Boxing Day 1909.

THE WELLINGTON HALL, Snargate Street, subsequently re-named the WELLINGTON CINEMA, became in February 1911, Dover's second establishment devoted to screening the early cinematograph pictures, while the DAY AND NIGHT OPEN-AIR CINEMA, Marine Parade, made a brief appearance in September 1911.

THE KING'S HALL, Biggin Street, was the first purpose-built cinema, opening in October 1911.

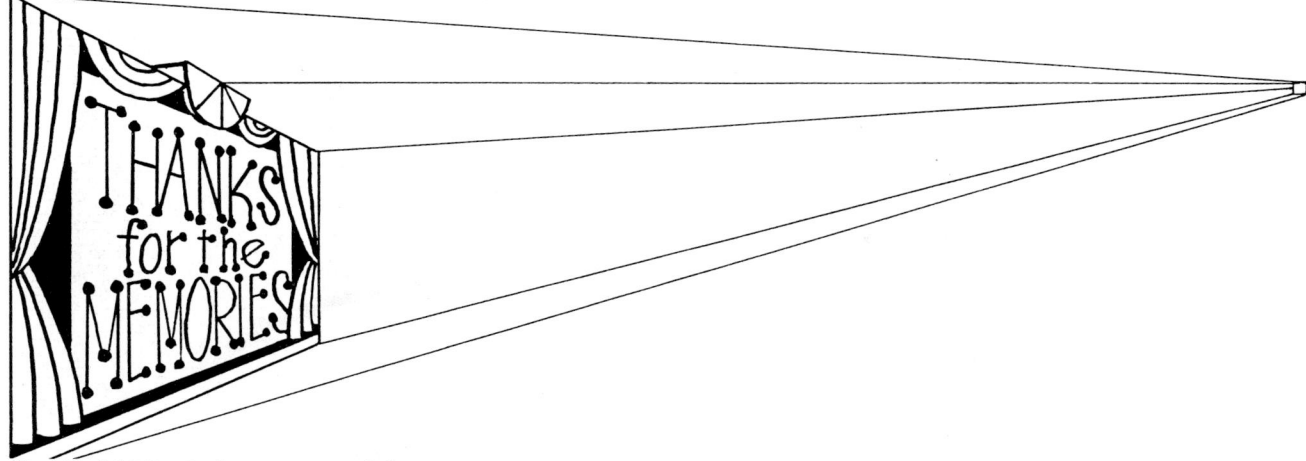

"In World War I, the patrons of the WELLINGTON HALL, the ROYAL HIPPODROME and the APOLLONIAN, could also enjoy the delights of Snargate Street. There was a huge transit camp by the docks, so all places of entertainment, including the 62 pubs and tattoo parlours, were very busy; it was the Soho of Dover!" *Mr F.P.*

The PEOPLE'S PICTURE PALACE's programme advertised in the DOVER TIMES of 27 February, 1911 (above) certainly did not lack variety, but presumably the photograph of the Apollonian Hotel was taken before the Picture Palace had established itself there in an upper room.

THE PALACE AND HIPPODROME was originally the EMPIRE THEATRE OF VARIETIES as shown in the above photograph, taken at the time of the coronation of King Edward VII, 9 August, 1901. The advertisement from the DOVER EXPRESS of 12 February, 1909, includes 'Palace and Hippodrome Popular Pictures by Raymond's Bio-Tableaux', otherwise Bioscope, the term in general use for the early cinema.

Royal Hippodrome
Snargate Street, Dover.
Managing Director—Mr. Sidney Winter.
Manager—Mr. E. Holford.
Telephone 325.

The Premier Theatre of Varieties in Dover.

Twice Nightly, 7.0 & 9.0.

MONDAY, FEB. 27th, and During Week.

Special starring engagement of
FANNY and HARRY DENT,
In their novel Comedy Melange, "THE INDIAN BOTTLE," including Sicilian and Russian numbers.

GITTO,
The Welsh double-voiced Vocalist.

MADGE MAY,
Dainty Comedienne.

HIPPODROME PICTURES.

FRED and LULU CAMPLIN,
In their latest success entitled, "A Dressing Room Interlude," direct from the London Pavilion.

THE QUAILS,
Speciality Artistes.

J. H. MAXWELL,
Comedian and Juggler.

Important engagement of that Lump of Fun—
LITTLE GANTY,
London's Popular Comedian.

Private Boxes 12/6 & 10/6 — Single Seats, 2/6	STALLS, 1/6 Early Doors, 1/9 If booked 2/-	Grand Circle. 1- Early Doors 1/3 If Booked 1/6
PIT 6d. Early Doors, 9d.	GALLERY 3d. Early Doors, 4d.	

Seats may be booked for the Boxes, Stalls, or Circle. No seats guaranteed unless booked. The right of refusing admission is reserved. No money returned.
The Theatre is heated on the most up-to-date principles during the cold weather.
Trams leave Northampton Street entrance at 8.46 and 10.50.

HIPPODROME PICTURES were regularly screened at the ROYAL HIPPODROME, see the DOVER EXPRESS advertisement of 24 November 1911, above. The first theatre on the site was opened in 1790 as the CLARENCE, but it was demolished and re-built as the TIVOLI THEATRE, opening in June 1897. Later its name was changed to the THEATRE ROYAL, but at the beginning of the century it became the ROYAL HIPPODROME, many famous artistes appearing there, particularly during the war years. The theatre closed after it was hit by a shell in September, 1944, and was demolished in January 1951. The photograph above shows the TIVOLI THEATRE and the one below shows the ROYAL HIPPODROME prior to demolition.

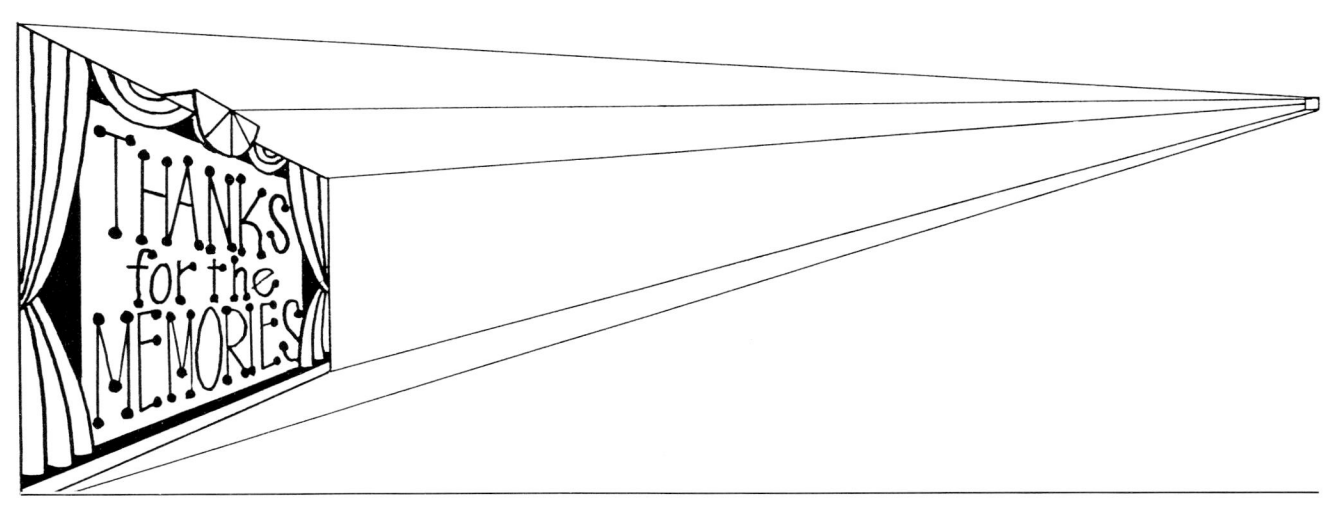

The Palace and Hippodrome

"When I was 8 years old, I paid tuppence to get in - we not only saw films but the Tiller Girls as well!" *Mr D, aged 79*

The Royal Hippodrome

"We thought nothing of walking from River to Snargate Street to see the music hall turns and the Hippodrome films. It cost 4d each to get in but we had to sit in the 'Gods' (balcony)." *Mr P.C.*

"In 1940, shortly before the show was due to start, a bomb exploded and made a mess of the stage. They dug out the piano and carried it to another building nearby, where the show was put on." *'Old Timer'*

"I can remember the Hippodrome films but, of course, my main recollection is of the variety artistes. I also enjoyed the orchestra there; I think a Mr Medhurst was the Musical Director. The staff of the Hippodrome were grand people and I recall seeing them, with their families, posing for a photo prior to their annual outing." *'Dovorian'*

STAFF OUTING, ROYAL HIPPODROME, c.1914. Photograph supplied by Musical Director's daughter, Mrs Una Savage nee Medhurst, whose brother Frank also played in the Hippodrome Orchestra when he was 17½ years old.

The Queen's Hall,
Queen Street

Dover's Zion Chapel opened as a place of worship in 1705 and was rebuilt in 1814. In the early 1900s it ceased to be a chapel and it is said that local tradesmen used to sharpen their knives on the tombstones there, before it was acquired by Electric Pictures (Dover) Ltd. and converted into THE QUEEN'S HALL, manager Mr H.C. Bishop. The picture palace opened on Boxing Day 1909, with a seating capacity of 450.

"The screen occupied the site of the pulpit, or the rear of the pulpit", recalls Mr J.V. Horn. "There were narrow side galleries on slender, unsafe-looking pillars, and a larger rear-end gallery, rather more substantial, which I suppose held the organ or the choir in its chapel days".

A programme of films advertised for the week commencing 27 February, 1911, included SILVER CLOUD'S SACRIFICE ('A Thrilling Western Story'), SHOOTING RAPIDS IN JAPAN ('A beautifully coloured Picture'), UNSELFISH LOVE, DETECTIVE IN PERIL and 'VIVAPHONE: Marvellous, Singing Pictures'. VIVAPHONE was an early sound-on-disc system invented by Cecil Hepworth, the British film pioneer, with the actors miming the words. For these delights, patrons paid 3d, 6d, or 1/-d, with children under 12 paying only 2d, 3d, or 6d. The programme was continuous from 6.30pm to 10.45pm, with Matinees on Wednesday and Saturday.

A St. Margaret's Bay resident recalls going to THE QUEEN'S HALL in 1912, paying 2d for a seat in the balcony. "There was a pianist located on the ground floor who played the accompaniment to the film, ARTIST'S MODEL, made by the Hepworth Company. I remember a garden scene (green tints used) during which the Model, for a moment or two, was seen completely nude. When she was chased by the villain, the film was tinted red. My friend and I, wishing to improve our schoolboy education, resolved to return on the next night to see the naked lady again; this we did."

During the silent-picture days, 'The Cinema nearest the Sea Front' did very well, particularly as its newspaper advertisements were far superior to the competition's, exhibiting a remarkable flair for presentation and detailed description.

In October, 1929, the first full-length talking pictures were screened in Dover, but THE QUEEN'S HALL were reluctant to install the expensive sound equipment. So silent pictures continued for about a year with the slogan SILENCE IS GOLDEN. But inevitably the change to talking pictures had to be made and THE QUEEN'S HALL switched to sound in October, 1930.

With five competing cinemas in Dover, including the GRANADA super-cinema, life became difficult for the non-circuit QUEEN'S HALL, this being reflected in changes of management which caused the 'Little House with the Big Programme' to open irregularly. Sadly, the cinema closed in April, 1933. During the war it was used as an army-boot repairs factory, eventually being acquired by a family firm of leather merchants. Subsequently the building was used as an amusement arcade until it was demolished in October 1974.

'SINGING PICTURES' were shown in this 1918 programme of films.

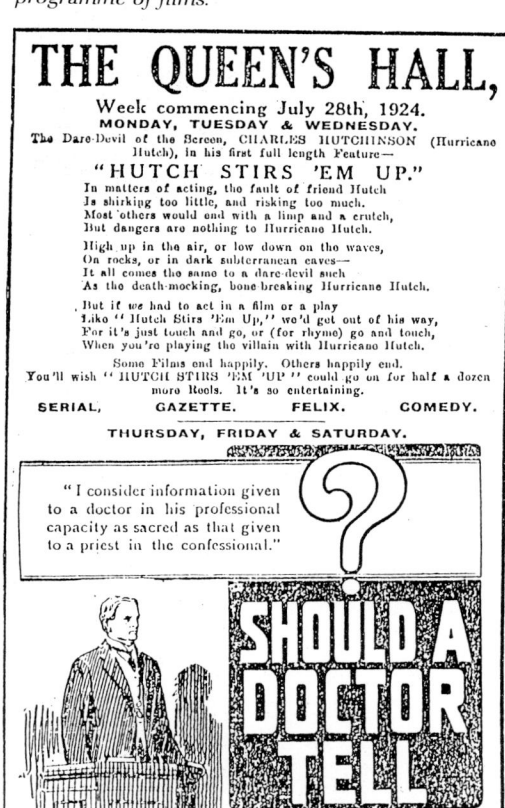

FASCINATING is the only word to describe this example of QUEEN'S HALL advertising in 1924.

ZION CHAPEL. As shown in the New Dover Guide, 1853.

AWAITING 'THE END'. This photograph, taken in September 1974, gives some idea of how the building appeared as THE QUEEN'S HALL cinema.

DEMOLITION, October 1974.

THE DOVER EXPRESS AND EAST KENT NEWS, FRIDAY, 26 DECEMBER, 1924.

THE QUEEN'S HALL.

Week commencing December 29th.

ALL THE WEEK

Continuous each day from 2.0 p.m.

Special Holiday Attraction!

The Management, in conjunction with Mr. Reginald Ford, proudly presents

"DOWN TO THE SEA IN SHIPS"

The WORLD'S GREATEST TRIUMPH, which created a PHENOMENAL SUCCESS at the PALACE THEATRE, LONDON.
Here is nature at her mightiest. A slip spells death, and events well nigh unbelievable take place apparently within a few feet of the astounded audience.

WHAT "DOWN TO THE SEA IN SHIPS" HAS DONE.

In LONDON it played for nine weeks at the PALACE THEATRE, and was taken off at the very height of its success, owing to the fact that a contract had been entered into to present another film at the Theatre, which could not be postponed, although heavy compensation was offered to cancel the contract.

MR. REGINALD FORD made a public offer in vain of £1,000 to £1,500 per week for another West End Theatre to continue this success.

It has since been shown for a further four weeks at the KENNINGTON THEATRE, LONDON, also with undoubted success.

Booked for two weeks' presentation at the CAMEO THEATRE, NEW YORK, so instantaneous and great a success was it that the film was retained for sixteen weeks, and in order to cope with the enormous and unprecedented demand for seats, the film was shown continuously from 10.30 a.m. till 11.30 p.m.

A WORLD'S RECORD.

It has proved one of the most successful pictures shown in PARIS.

Approximate Times of Showing   ...   ...   3 p.m.   6 p.m.   9 p.m.
FREE LIST ENTIRELY SUSPENDED.

WHAT THE PRESS SAYS.

"The picture carries with it the wind and salt of the open sea, and has some claim to be considered the most impressive film of the year."—*Daily Mail.*

"More exciting than anything that has been shown in this country before. We see a bull whale actually harpooned, and are shown its extraordinary struggles afterwards. These pictures have been taken at great personal risk, and are beyond praise."—*The Times.*

"The big thrill is a fight between a ninety-ton whale and a boatful of harpooners. The mutiny and fight aboard ship have also been very well done."—*Daily Mirror.*

"From the hour when the white-winged, square-rigged barque—a grand sight—sails into the sunrise, to the day when she returns, storm-swept and battered, the spectator is held enthralled. If all films were as good as 'DOWN TO THE SEA IN SHIPS,' criticism would be a sinecure."—*Daily Express.*

WHAT FAMOUS PEOPLE THINK.

SIR ARTHUR CONAN DOYLE says:—
"I was a whaleman before I was an author, and the scenes in 'DOWN TO THE SEA IN SHIPS' brought vanished days of my youth very vividly back to me. I have never seen anything finer than the episode of the taking of the whale, and in sure adventurous excitement I cannot believe that it will ever be excelled in the whole history of the Cinema industry. I hope it has the success it deserves."

C. R. O. NEVINSON, the distinguished artist, says:
"This is the film that every boy and girl must be taken to see, lest its parents stand for ever disgraced. As thrilling as Stevenson at his best. And much more entertaining than pantomime."

CHARLES CHAPLIN, the renowned film actor, writes:
"There can be no quibbling about choosing such a picture as 'DOWN TO THE SEA IN SHIPS' as among the best of the year."

N.B.—The celebrated "LOVE WALTZ" featured in "DOWN TO THE SEA IN SHIPS" can be obtained at Messrs. GOULDEN & WIND'S, 5, Cannon St.

PRICES OF ADMISSION   -   -   4d., 6d., 8d., 1/2.
Children Half-price to all parts at Matinees only.   No Half-price whatever to evening performances.
Remember the times.   Continuous each day from 2.0 p.m.

WATCH FOR OUR NEXT BIG WEEK:—Syd. Walker in "OLD BILL THROUGH THE AGES," and Norma Talmadge in "ASHES OF VENGEANCE."

THE BIG SELL. Another example of QUEEN'S HALL advertising in 1924. In the 'What Famous People Think' panel on the right of the display, Charles Chaplin's tribute to the film reads: "There is no quibbling about choosing such a picture as DOWN TO THE SEA IN SHIPS as among the best of the year."

Wellington Hall
(later Wellington Cinema), Snargate Street

ON PARADE, 1911. The staff of the WELLINGTON HALL.

Dating back to c.1857, the WELLINGTON HALL in 1911 became Dover's second establishment fully devoted to screening the early cinematograph pictures, although on the Grand Opening Night on 25 February, 1911, the invited audience of 400 were also entertained by Professors Lenton and Bertram, in their 'marvellous Thought Reading Entertainment, as given on six occasions before Members of the Royal Family'. As for the films, they included such epics as *BRONCHO BILL'S REDEMPTION, WILFUL PEGGY, DOLLY IN DANGER, FATHER BUYS A CHIMNEY POT* and *FOOLSHEAD AND FOOTBALL*. After the Grand Opening, the hall was open on the following Monday, matinees from 3 to 4.30pm, evenings 6.30 to 10.45pm. The prices were 3d, 6d, and 1/-d, children 2d, 3d, and 6d.

WELLINGTON HALL,
SNARGATE STREET, DOVER.

Shanly's Electric Animated Pictures.

GRAND
Invitation Opening Night,
Admission by TICKET ONLY.

SATURDAY, FEBRUARY 25th.

Programme.
A DAY IN MICK'S LIFE.
WIFFLES TRIES WORK.
BRONCHO BILL'S REDEMPTION.
WILFUL PEGGY.
FATHER BUYS A CHIMNEY POT.
DOLLY IN DANGER.
MOTHER'S SON & BROTHER'S WARD.
FOOLSHEAD AND FOOTBALL.

SPECIAL FOR THIS NIGHT ONLY!
Prof. Lenton and Bertram,
In their marvellous Conjuring and Thought Reading Entertainment, as given on six occasions before Members of the Royal Family, and at all principal London Halls.

THE HALL WILL BE OPEN TO THE PUBLIC ON MONDAY.
MATINEE 3 to 4.30 p.m.
EVENING 6.30 to 10.45.

Prices: 3d., 6d., and 1/-. Children, 2d., 3d., and 6d.

GRAND OPENING NIGHT advertisement in the DOVER EXPRESS of 24 February, 1911. No less than 8 films plus a variety turn.

The WELLINGTON HALL soon became a very popular venue for the citizens of Dover, although they must have been puzzled at the changes in the admission charges from the original 3d, 6d, and 1/-d. For example in the Dover Town Guide of 1914, the prices are given as 2d, 4d and 6d and in the Dover Express of 13 December, 1918, they are shown as 3d, 5d and 9d, although it is noted that the latter includes tax!

Quite an innovation in November 1911, was the screening of *LIFE ON THE OXO CATTLE FARMS*, advertisements for which announced 'There is a very big demand for this film and we have been fortunate enough to secure it for our patrons'. Was this the first (concealed) advertising film? Did the management receive any hand-out from Oxo Ltd. for showing it? Or were free samples of the famous cube given away as patrons left the cinema?

During the first World War the WELLINGTON HALL did record business, Sundays between 5 to 9pm being reserved for 'Soldiers and Sailors only', a typical programme in December 1918 including *OTRONTO, KING OF THIEVES* (A great Detective Drama, in Five Parts), *THE LASS OF THE LUMBERLANDS* (Episode XIV), and the comedy *WHAT'S SAUCE FOR THE GOOSE*. In addition, the PICTORIAL NEWS was shown at each programme.

After the war, the theatre became the WELLINGTON CINEMA, not least of its attractions being the resident pianist, Emma Beer, who sat with a brass-ringed curtain round her and the piano. Into this arena, when the lights went down, descended a shower of apple cores and empty sweet bags from the hands of giggling school children. This was gross ingratitude, for every child entering the cinema was given a bag of sweets or chopped-up Dover rock. However, the appearance of the huge front-door attendant, resplendant with rows of medals on his chest, soon restored order, the offenders settling down on the hard wooden forms which were then the standard seating.

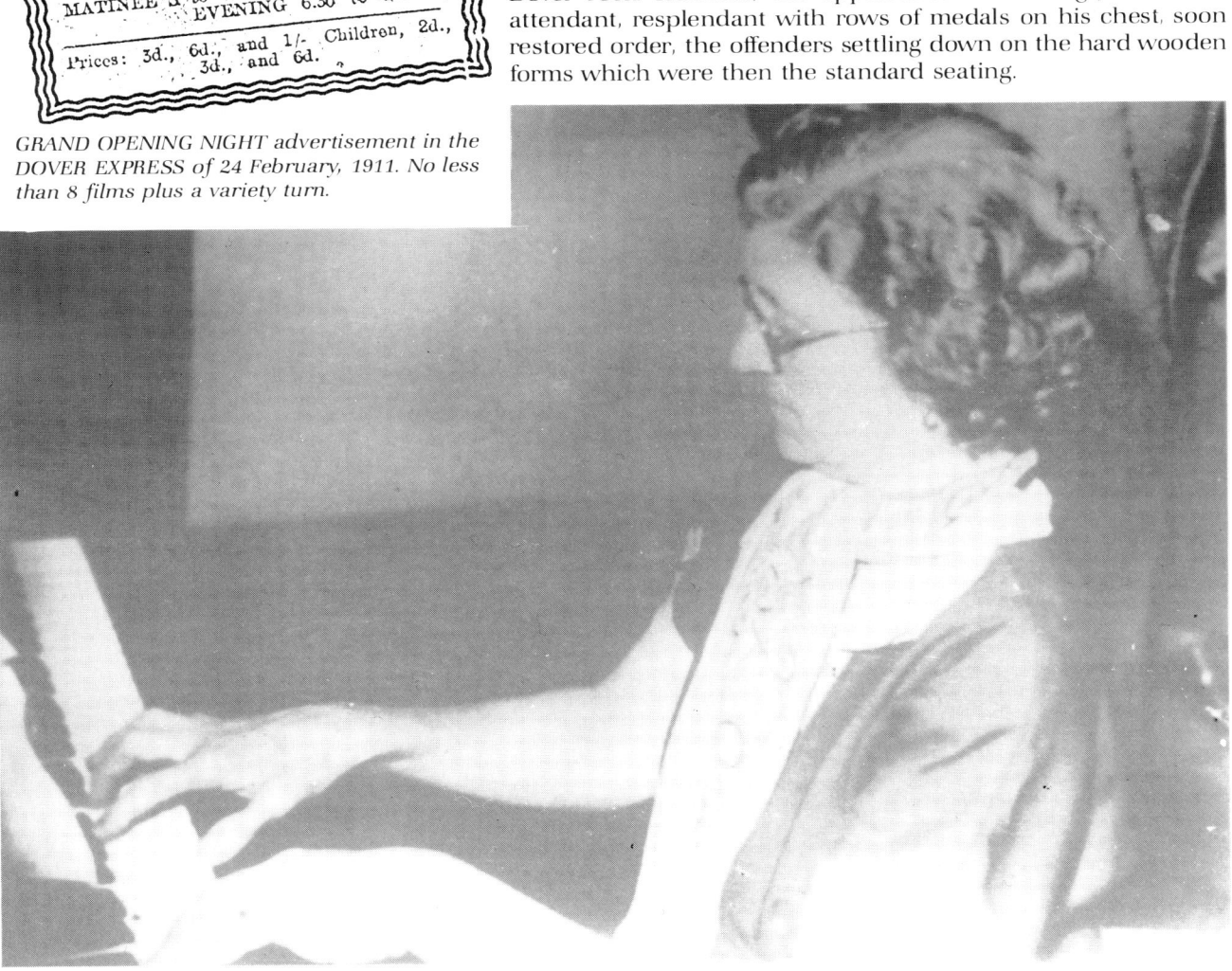

EMMA BEER, pianist at the WELLINGTON CINEMA: apple cores were thrown into her brass-ringed curtain area, while she was playing for the silent films.

The projection point at the WELLINGTON CINEMA was very low, so that when the patron passed through a mysterious set of curtains which he reached after carefully negotiating a sloping floor, his head would be caught by the beam and its shadow would appear on the screen, the audience shouting 'SIT DOWN'. But it was all part of the fun of going to the pictures in those days and certainly did not affect attendances.

In October 1929 the WELLINGTON CINEMA made the momentous change to talking pictures, installing an all-British sound system at considerable expense. The opening film for the talkie-era was advertised as: 'The Greatest all-melody film made, Dover's first 100% talkie - MORTON DOWNEY in *MOTHER'S BOY*'. However, like the QUEEN'S HALL, the WELLINGTON ran into difficulties in the early thirties, the cinema changing hands in February 1930. In May the WELLINGTON became the PAVILION; in October the name was changed to the PAVILION CINEMA AND PALAIS DE DANCE, when dancing was on Monday, Tuesday and Wednesday from 8pm to 11pm, with films being shown for the rest of the week. Even this formula did not prove successful and in November the dancing was dropped, leaving films shown every day as for other Dover cinemas. But by the end of the year business was so bad that the theatre finally closed.

BEEFING UP THE SHOW?
This advertisement appeared in the DOVER TIMES of 10 November, 1911.

COMFORT FOR THE TROOPS
'Open on Sundays, 5 till 9pm, Soldiers and Sailors only' reads this advert in the DOVER EXPRESS of 13 December, 1918.

LADIES' POCKET MIRRORS *were given away at the WELLINGTON CINEMA, with the advertisement shown here on the reverse side.*

> # DAY and NIGHT
> # OPEN-AIR CINEMA
> MARINE PARADE, (Adjoining the County Rink,) DOVER, will open on
> ## SATURDAY, SEPTEMBER 9th, 1911
> At 3.30 O'clock.
> ## DAYLIGHT PICTURES
> FIRST TIME IN ENGLAND.
>
> THREE SHOWS A DAY, Afternoon 3.30. Evening 7 and 9.
> PRICES 6d., and 3d. Children Half-price to 6d. Seats.
> Latest & Most Perfect Pictures. Change Three Times Weekly.
> PATHE'S GAZETTE, with the Latest News Illustrated.
>
> COMFORTABLE CHAIRS.   FRESH AIR.   HIGH-CLASS AMUSEMENT
>
> ## SPECIAL PROGRAMME SUNDAYS AT 8 p.m.

Dover's Open-Air Cinema

adjoining the County Rink, Marine Parade, opened for business on 9 September 1911. It stayed only a few weeks before moving on to new venues, a splendid example of private enterprise by the showmen of that time who did much to popularise the Bioscope. It is interesting to note that an Open-Air Cinema opened in Folkestone on 29 May, 1912 (see Folkestone section of this book) but whether it was under the same management as the Dover cinema is not known.

THE COUNTY RINK, alongside which was located the OPEN-AIR CINEMA, was on the Marine Parade at the East Cliffs end.

King's Hall
(later Gaumont), Biggin Street

The KING'S HALL was Dover's first purpose-built cinema and the Grand Opening was on 21 October 1911 when a special programme of Kinemacolor and other splendid pictures was screened. Miss Lilian Allen sang and music was provided by a resident orchestra; in addition Dover's first cinema organ, a 'Gregorian', performed, much to the delight of the capacity audience. The following week patrons were to enjoy four films in Kinemacolor: SUNSET IN EGYPT, A DAY AT HENLEY, REVIEW OF TROOPS BY HM THE KING and NORTH WEST MOUNTED POLICE, plus the latest issue of Gaumont Graphic and other items.

After the spartan comforts of the WELLINGTON HALL and the QUEEN'S HALL, the new cinema must have come as quite a revelation to Dover's filmgoers. There was a reception hall cum foyer 'handsomely decorated, admirably fitted for light refreshments and afternoon teas' leading to the auditorium 100" long, 60" wide and 30" high. The absence of supporting roof columns ensured that patrons had an unobstructed view of the screen. Access to the balcony was through a narrow passage on the right hand side of the foyer where a separate paybox was situated. Here metal tokens were issued by the cashier in lieu of tickets, the tokens being handed to the usherette at the top of the stairs who then placed them in a box for collection and re-use. Children loved to carry the tokens and hand them over to the usherette.

The KING's HALL seated 800 people in varying degrees of comfort. Opera tub chairs accommodated 100 in the lounge (1/-d), 400 could sit in tip-up armchairs in the stalls (6d), and 300 in tip-ups in the balcony (3d). Lounge patrons could also enjoy the privilege of relaxing in a semi-circular drawing room at the rear of the hall, where there were comfortable armchairs, occasional tables and even a cosy fireplace. Certainly the proprietors, a local syndicate, could claim that designer A.H. Steele's cinema, built at a cost of around £8,000, was the most luxurious picture palace within a 75 miles radius.

KING'S HALL,
BIGGIN STREET, DOVER.

Proprietors: - The Dover Picture Palace Co., Ltd.
Managing Director: - - - H. R. Geddes.

Dover's PREMIER Picture Playhouse

ALWAYS A STAR PROGRAMME
OF THE
Finest Pictures, the Best Vocalists and Entertainers and Most Varied Music.

SPLENDID ORCHESTRA.

Twice Nightly - 6.30 & 8.45

For Matinees and full Programme, see Bills.

POPULAR PRICES.

SPECIAL REDUCTION FOR SCHOOLS, CHILDREN, and PARTIES.

TELEPHONE No. 580.

FILMS plus VARIETY ACTS were at the KING'S HALL in 1914, as this advert in the DOVER TOWN GUIDE shows.

Sketch of metal token used at the King's Hall in lieu of tickets for balcony seats.

CONVENIENT TRAINS TO DOVER were an incentive for Folkestone residents to visit the KING'S HALL, this advert appearing in the FOLKESTONE GAZETTE of 1 June 1912.

KING'S HALL, BIGGIN ST., DOVER.
Proprietors:—The Dover Picture Palace Co., Ltd.
DOVER'S PALATIAL PICTURE PLAYHOUSE.
WEEK COMMENCING MONDAY, 3rd JUNE.
Special and Expensive Engagement of
THE ZANCIGS
(JULIUS and AGNES).
The Most Marvellous of all Mind Readers.
"TWO MINDS WITH BUT A SINGLE THOUGHT."
Their Telepathic Display is as wonderful as when their marvellous entertainment made such an astounding sensation in London, when the ALHAMBRA THEATRE was CROWDED OUT for 15 CONSECUTIVE WEEKS by appreciative audiences, absolutely mystified by the wonderful display given.
Mr. and Mme. Zancig had the unique honour of being commanded to Sandringham by His Late Majesty KING EDWARD VII, before whom they appeared no less than THREE TIMES.
EXCLUSIVE APPEARANCE OF
DAISY HICKS,
London's Popular Comedienne.
SPLENDID PROGRAMME OF UP-TO-DATE PICTURES.
THE BEST OF HIGH-CLASS MUSIC BY THE RENOWNED "KING'S HALL" ORCHESTRA.
WEDNESDAY AND SATURDAY, SPECIAL MATINEES AT 2 45.
TWO PERFORMANCES EACH EVENING AT 6.30 AND 8.45.
Popular Prices: Lounge, 1/- Stalls, 6d. Balcony, 3d. Children 6d. & 2d
Seats booked in advance to Lounge and Stalls, extra charge 3d.
TELEPHONE No. 580 DOVER.
Convenient trains to Dover from Central Station, 28, 2.52, 6 0, 6.24, 7.38, 8.21. From Dover Harbour, 6.30, 8.27, 9.50, 10.27, 11.4.

THE KING'S HALL, Dover's first purpose built cinema, was not only spacious but had the merit of being without any supporting pillars to obstruct patrons' view of the screen.

LILIAN GISH, renowned star of the silent films, was a favourite with the early KINGS'S HALL audiences. Her performance in the 1919 film BROKEN BLOSSOMS was considered extraordinary, perhaps due to pioneering director D.W. Griffith whose masterpiece was THE BIRTH OF A NATION (1915).

KING'S HALL

Biggin Street, Dover.

Lessees ... Harry Day's Amusements, Limited.
Managing Director - HARRY DAY. 'Phone: 580

MONDAY, DEC. 16th, 1918.

Special and attractive Engagement of—
MISS META FOX, Operatic Soprano.

MONDAY, TUESDAY and WEDNESDAY.
Grand Screen Drama, in Five Parts—
THE MARIONETTES,
A really artistic play of surpassing interest
Clara Keinhall Young as the heroine.
LUKE'S LOVE DREAM,
A Whirlwind of Comedy, in Two Reels.
THE RACE TO THE DRAWBRIDGE,
Thrilling Drama; featuring the famous film
actress, Helen Holmes.

THURSDAY, FRIDAY and SATURDAY.
Episode I. (in Two Parts) of the Serial Supreme—
THE HOUSE OF HATE,
Pearl White and Antonio Moreno in 20
Episodes. First Instalment, entitled—
"THE HOODED TERROR."
A ROUGH TURKEY TROT,
Rollicking Keystone Comedy.
Fine Photo Drama, in Five Parts—
THE HOUSE OF CARDS,
A Story of Heart Interest; featuring Catherine Calvert and Frank Mills.

Prices:—1/6 (and tax, 4d.); 1/- (and tax, 3d.)
6d. (and tax, 2d.); 3d. (and tax, 1d.).
Continuous Performances:—
Mon., Wed., and Sat., 2.30 to 10. Tues., Thurs.
and Fri., 4.15 to 10. No Half-Price after 3 p.m.
Children's Matinee—Saturday, Half-price, 3 p.m.
HIGH-CLASS TEA ROOMS,
OPEN DAILY, from 11 a.m. FIRST FLOOR.

Although the KING'S HALL was launched as a full-time cinema, within a year or two Harry Day's Amusements Ltd. acquired the theatre and films took second place to live entertainment. The architect had been generous in providing a 36'-deep stage and this, combined with a proscenium width of 32', enabled almost any type of stage production to be mounted. There were also nine dressing rooms, an exceptionally generous provision for the artistes. But in 1914, films did return for good, at first supporting variety acts and then alternating film and live shows.

When talkies hit Dover in October, 1929, the immediate reaction of the KING'S HALL was to have nothing to do with the new medium, particulary as the theatre was planning a pantomime over the Christmas period and thereafter a series of stage plays. However, after a three-month theatrical season with a weekly change of programme, RCA sound equipment was installed and the first sound films were screened in the KING'S HALL in April, 1931.

Later in 1931, Dover Entertainments Ltd. became lessees of the cinema, with Managing Director L.G.T. Harrison Ainsworth making many improvements to the hall, notably raising the seating capacity to 1050. Then came calamity. On 29 December, 1937, the KING'S HALL was totally destroyed by fire. Not until 1940 was the cinema re-built and then it was promptly requisitioned by the Royal Navy to train recruits in gunnery procedures.

MIXED BAG. On 16 December, 1918, the films were supported by an Operatic Soprano.

QUO VADIS was an Italian-made epic of the early silent cinema and the KING'S HALL screened it on 16 June 1913, making it something of an occasion. A special programme leaflet was produced, measuring 11½" x 6", the front of which (reproduced above) showed scenes from the film, the reverse side providing detailed write-ups of each of the six parts of the film, with such headings as THE DAWN OF LOVE, THE COURT OF NERO AT AUTURIN, THE BURNING OF ROME and THE DEATH OF NERO.

THE KING'S HALL
DOVER.

Programme

Prices of Admission.—Fauteuils and Settees, 1 6. Early Door 2/-, or Reserved, 2/-; Saturdays (2nd House only) Bank Holidays & Special Nights 2/-; Orc. Stalls, 1/-, Early Door, 1/3, if Booked in advance, 1/6; Pit Stalls, 6d. Early Door or if Booked in advance, 9d.; Circle, 3d. Early Door or Booked in advance 6d. All Children must be paid for. Also Babies in arms.

Twice Nightly at 6.45 & 8.55

KING'S HALL
DOVER.

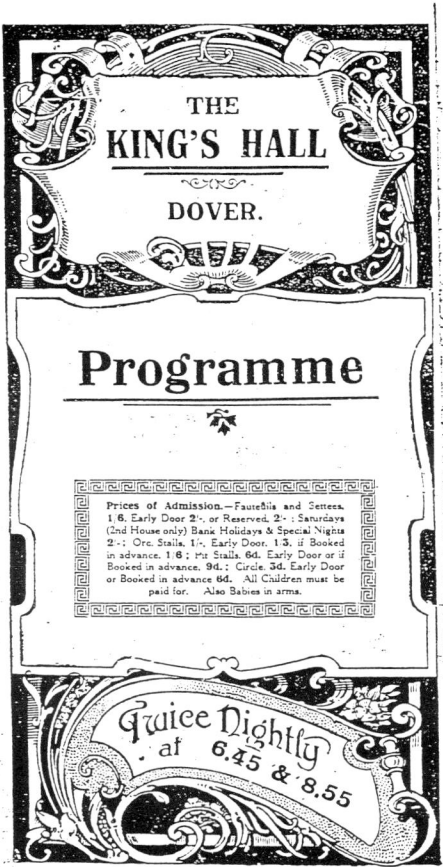

Lessees .... Harry Day's Amusements, Ltd.
General Manager .... Mr. Harry Day.
Acting Resident Manager .... Mr. Percy M. Calder.
Musical Director .... Mr. William MacDonald.
Telephone—580 Dover.

Monday, July 20th, 1914.

1 OVERTURE

2 JOSIE HENRY, Comedienne

3 FRED WRIGHT, Comedian

4 FIVE PETLEYS, In their Great and Refined Comedy Aerial Production

5 BRULL & HEMSLEY, In their Latest Production—THE KNUT, THE GIRL AND THE EGG. In "URALIARTY" Two Scenes

6 LEW LAKE & CO., in his Screamingly Funny and Sensational Episode "THE BLOOMSBURY BURGLARS" Special Scenery and Effects

7 JEWEL ST. LEGER. The Burlesque Actress with Vocal and Musical Talent

8 THE TOPICAL GAZETTE Portrayed in the Bioscope Different Series will be continued Twice Weekly.

9 LEW LAKE & CO., in the Sequel Story "MY PAL JERRY" Special and Elaborate Scenery SEE THE PRISON MUTINY

Special Picture Matinee Every Saturday at 2.45
Special Reduced Prices 1s., 5d., 4d.–2d. Children 1d., 2d., 3d. 6d.

LADIES ARE RESPECTFULLY REQUESTED TO REMOVE THEIR HATS.

In the Interest of Public Health this building is daily disinfected with Jeye's Fluid.

LADIES ARE RESPECTFULLY REQUESTED TO REMOVE THEIR HATS

This delightful KING'S HALL programme (top) for 20 July, 1914, has been reduced to half-size.

Inside were full details of the variety acts, supported by 'Item 8: THE TOPICAL GAZETTE, Portrayed in the Bioscope'. The remainder of the programme's interior consisted of advertisements for local firms (not shown here), and a note about the Management's desire 'to keep entertainment free from all suggestiveness, vulgarity and any word or actions with a double meaning'.

The Management endeavour to keep this entertainment free from all suggestiveness, vulgarity and any word or actions with a double meaning but should anything escape their notice they will be more than obliged if their patrons will immediately draw the attention of the Local Manager to same. Mr. Harry Day will be pleased if the patrons of the King's Hall have any suggestions they could make that would add to the convenience of the patrons of this establishment if they will make same in writing addressed to

Mr. Harry Day,
Effingham House,
Arundel Street,
Strand, London, W.C.

KING'S HALL — THIS IS NOW ODEON — DOVER
Telephone 1344

GRAND OPENING
MONDAY, JULY 14th, at 6 p.m.
BY
THE RIGHT WORSHIPFUL THE MAYOR OF DOVER
(Councillor A. T. Goodfellow, J.P.)

Personal Appearance of
DAVID FARRAR
STAR OF "FRIEDA"

BAND OF THE ROYAL MARINES
ON THE STAGE

TUESDAY to SATURDAY   DOORS OPEN 12.45 p.m.

WOULD YOU TAKE
FRIEDA
INTO YOUR HOME?

EALING STUDIOS PRESENT
THE FILM THAT PUTS THE QUESTION with
DAVID FARRAR · GLYNIS JOHNS
FLORA ROBSON · ALBERT LIEVEN
and the new Swedish star
MAI ZETTERLING

PRODUCED BY MICHAEL BALCON DIRECTED BY BASIL DEARDEN
SCREENPLAY BY ANGUS MacPHAIL AND RONALD MILLAR
2.20   5.20   4.20

Chips Rafferty in BUSH CHRISTMAS (U)
1.0   4.0   7.0

The Grand Re-opening of the KING'S HALL under the ODEON banner took place on 14 July 1947, with some rousing music from the band of the Royal Marines and the personal appearance of David Farrar, star of the opening film *FRIEDA*. The opening ceremony was conducted by the Mayor of Dover, Cllr. A.T. Goodfellow JP, indicating the importance then attached to cinemas as a vital part of the local community.

The new manager was Frank E. Brissenden who was to see the cinema's name changed to the GAUMONT in January, 1951, and finally its closure on 26 November 1960, with a film called *THE TIME MACHINE*. Time had indeed run out for the GAUMONT and in 1961 the hall opened for Bingo.

STAFF OF THE KING'S HALL, about 1930. This photograph was taken at the entrance to the cinema and includes the manager, assistant manager, projectionist, doorman, usherettes, page boys and cashiers. The uniformed staff were inspected daily by the manager to ensure that a high standard of dress and general appearance was maintained, the neat white gloves tucked into epaulettes adding to the general effect. Cinema staffs were proud of their cinemas, many of them working long hours for small wages.

BRIEF INTERLUDE. In 1933 somebody had the curious idea of changing the theatre's name to KING'S CINEMA. Although the background of the White Cliffs in this Dover Express advert of 28 July, 1933, had some appeal, the old name was soon restored and continued until the 1951 change to GAUMONT.

WHAT A DIFFERENCE A WEEK MAKES. On 5 January, 1951, it was the KING'S HALL; a week later it was the GAUMONT.

QUEUEING ALL PARTS. Whatever the name, Dovorians still stood in line for vacant seats, at least when these photographs were taken.

CITY ACROSS THE RIVER was shown at the KING'S HALL 1949 (left) and

THE GREATEST SHOW ON EARTH at the GAUMONT in 1952 (below).

Thanks for the Memories

The King's Hall

"I think it was at the KING'S HALL that I first saw Theda Bara, from which time forth I tried to see every picture in which she appeared. My mother thought she was a very bad example for we youngsters, a home-breaker if there ever was one. But my mother was hooked too!" *Mrs C.*

"The Manager, Harry Day, used to stand at the entrance to the cinema with a flower in the button-hole of his jacket. If you caught him without the flower in place, he would give you half-a-crown." *Mr T.D.*

THEDA BARA, real name Theodosia Goodman, was the screen's original vamp and the product of an extremely skilful press agent. Her first film was A FOOL THERE WAS (1915) and she went on to make some 40 more films. She is shown in the photograph above in a typical train-top scene.

"I liked the KING'S HALL because when I was little I was allowed to take the metal tickets to give to the usherette upstairs and then watch her put them in a big wooden box until next time." *Mrs S.*

"The programme consisted of two full-length films plus Pathé Gazette or Movietone News. If the gallery became too noisy, the more vocal clients were ejected by the uniformed attendants." *Mr M.*

"One day in 1940, I watched an aerial dogfight as I stood outside the KING'S HALL. When I glanced at the poster advertising the current film, I saw it was *HELL'S ANGELS!*" *Mr J.*

"I remember in 1933 that an 'Old Crock' tour started from outside the KING'S HALL. A Mr Cozzi was to travel through the U.K. and then Africa in a 30-year old 6hp single-cylinder Humber to prove the reliability of British products. The Universal News were there to film the start (it was a Wednesday morning) and said the newsreel would be shown in the KING'S HALL the following Monday, Tuesday and Wednesday; it was!" *Mr D.E.*

"The KING'S HALL had double-seats at the back of the stalls, and these were ideal for courting couples. I always found the absence of an arm-rest between me and my girlfriend(s) a major contribution to satisfactory body-language." *Mr B.H.*

The Queen's Hall

"The cinema was spotlessly clean and when I was a schoolboy was entirely manned by the Whittle family - father, mother and two daughters. It was mother who provided the piano accompaniment to the films. I went regularly to follow such serials as *JUDEX* and *EXPLOITS OF ELAINE*. These serials left the heroine in a serious predicament with the closing words TO BE CONTINUED NEXT WEEK." *Mr W.T.M.*

"On General Election Nights, after the last film had been shown, they used to put voting results on the screen, with patrons jeering or cheering according to their political views." *Mrs S.*

"In the days of the silent films they used sound effects very cleverly. Sheets of tin were waved to imitate the sound of thunder and special lights were used to simulate lightning." *Mr F.P.*

"I used to go to the Saturday matinees for children. At one time the admission charge was one 2lb jamjar or two 1lb jamjars!" *Mr D.*

"They showed surprisingly good films there, including the early cartoons of *FELIX THE CAT*. The box office handed you a programme when you went in, but of course you couldn't read it until the interval." *Mr H.*

The Twenties

DOVER gained two new cinemas in the Twenties: the purpose-built BUCKLAND PICTURE HOUSE and the PLAZA, a conversion. By the end of the Twenties there were five cinemas in Dover (population c.41,000) with a sixth under construction, the total seating capacity being more than sufficient to provide seats each week for every man, woman and child in the town.

Buckland Picture House
(later the REGENT), London Road

The site chosen for Dover's fourth cinema was at Buckland, on the outskirts of Dover on the main road to Canterbury. Although it was an out-of-town location, it was much appreciated by residents in the area and by those who lived in River, a rapidly-growing suburb of Dover nearby. The building when completed looked more like a bank than a place of entertainment, although there could be no doubt as to the nature of the building because THE BUCKLAND PICTURE HOUSE was cast into the cement facade for all to see.

Designed by Worsfold and Hayward of Dover, the cinema consisted of a main entrance, vestibule with cloakroom and offices, and an auditorium seating 533 on one level. "The decorations, although plain, have a pleasing appearance" commented the local press, with a certain lack of enthusiasm. The cinema opened on 27 December, 1920, and in the following fifteen years lead a somewhat chequered existence, passing through a large number of entrepreneurial hands and driving at least one lessee to bankruptcy.

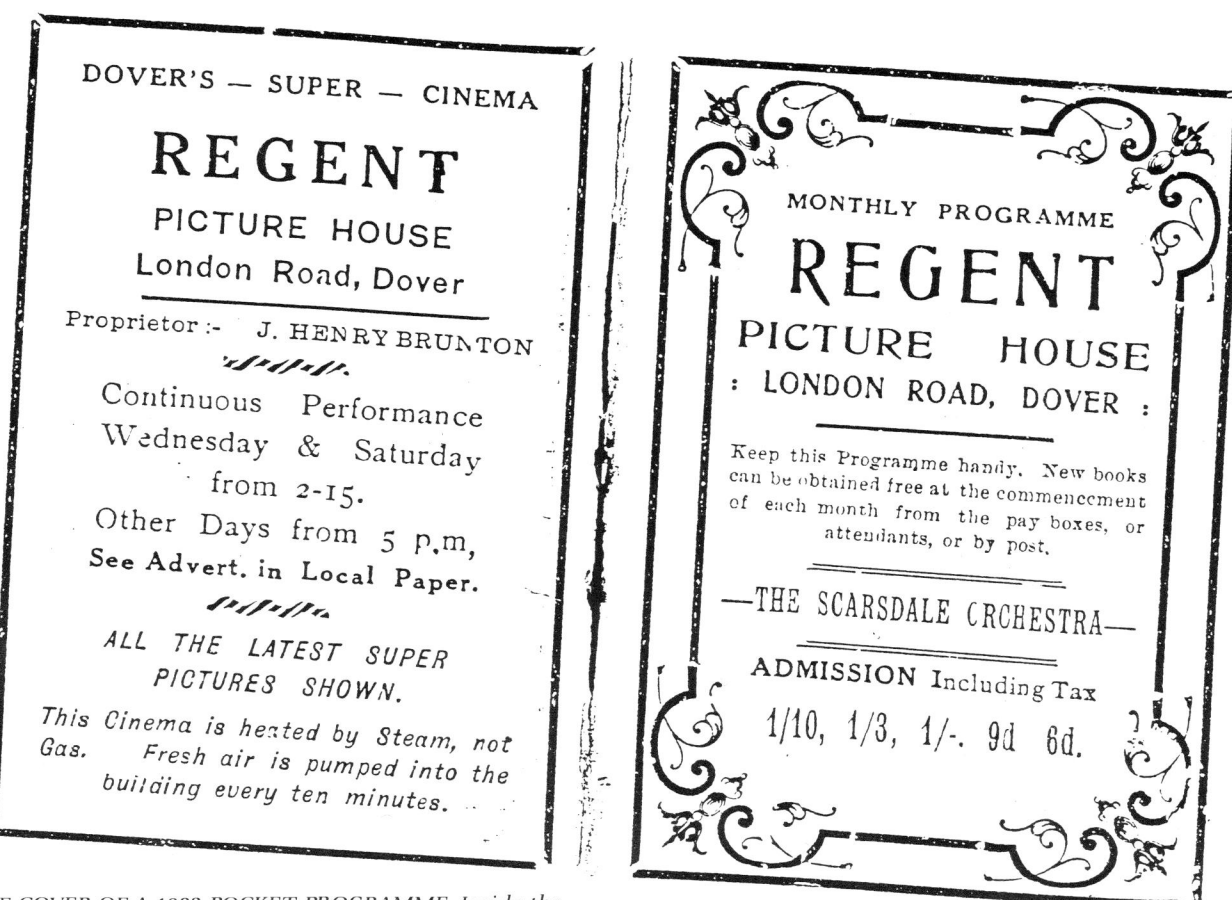

THE COVER OF A 1923 POCKET PROGRAMME. Inside the forthcoming attractions included: Norma Talmage in WITHIN THE LAW, THE MYSTERY OF FU MANCHU (a serial), Lon Chaney in A BLIND BARGAIN and Pola Negri in MAD LOVE.

There was a change of name to REGENT PICTURE HOUSE in 1923 and sound-equipment was installed in December 1930. In between, the cinema closed, re-opened and then closed again. When, in 1934, the property came into the hands of showman Arthur Phillips, it looked as though the REGENT would be secure at last. But by now the GRANADA super cinema was dominating the entertainment scene and the little REGENT was hopelessly outclassed. Arthur Phillips, following the maxim "If you can't beat 'em, join 'em", ordered plans to be drawn up for the new REGENT to be erected on the site of the old. So the cinema closed on 31st May 1936 and was soon demolished; work on the foundations for the new cinema followed immediately.

HOW IT USED TO BE. The BUCKLAND PICTURE HOUSE at the height of its popularity.

DISTRIBUTION OF EASTER EGGS, 1933, to the cinema's junior patrons, who now have to call it THE REGENT. It is a photograph which demonstrates once again the important role played by cinemas in the life of the community.

The POOR KIDDIES TREAT, January 1934, at THE REGENT. Seven hundred of Dover's poorer children were invited to the two-hour entertainment, on the Saturday morning. Afterwards, sweets, fruit and balloons were given to them. This was the second occasion that manager Arthur Phillips had entertained poor children, a similar show being held on Boxing Day. The upper photograph clearly shows the fascia reading BUCKLAND PICTURE HOUSE, with the new name REGENT on a framework to the fore. Both photographs are eloquent testimonies to the social significance of the cinema in those days and the sea of young faces in the lower photograph is most moving.

Plaza
(later Essoldo), Cannon Street

GEORGE ARLISS was a frequent visitor to the PLAZA CINEMA, where he was able to see himself as DISRAELI (above). In other films he played such parts as Voltaire, Cardinal Richelieu and Alexander Hamilton. He also appeared in OLD ENGLISH, THE GREEN GODDESS and DR SYN.

Although talking pictures had arrived, it was as a silent cinema with the screen painted on the rear wall, that the PLAZA opened for business on 1 July 1929. A spokesman explained that they had decided to show silent films because the provision of sound apparatus was largely in the hands of the Western Electric Company of the USA who demanded 50% of their profits; this would mean increasing the seat prices which they were not prepared to do.

The man responsible for converting a bus garage into a modern cinema seating 1200 was A.H. Steel, architect of the rival KING'S HALL not far away. Incorporated in the property was part of a disused hotel and the paybox stood in the well where the lift was originally located. The auditorium lay behind the properties facing Cannon Street where the main, narrow, shopfront entrance was situated. Another entrance was in New Street. A flight of steps led to the entrance hall which opened out into a café on one side (later taken over by the Friern Manor Icecream and Catering Co.) and a lounge on the other with the doors at the rear leading to the auditorium. Apart from a private box at the back, seating was at one level, no balcony being provided although it was stated that a balcony could be added later if required. A feature of the cinema was the sliding roof, which 'in real sultry weather would slide back and allow the vitiated atmosphere to escape'. The projection box was outside the building, perhaps to comply with fire regulations. In addition to the resident PLAZA orchestra, an organpian was installed, this being a combination upright grand piano and an electrically-blown high power reed organ manufactured by Whomes Ltd. of Bexley Heath.

The opening programme of silent films included Madge Bellamy in *DOES MOTHER KNOW BEST?* and Betty Compson in *LIFE'S MOCKERY*, all for 6d, 1/-d or 1/6d, with lower prices at matinees. 'Real Talkies' arrived at the PLAZA in November 1929, just four months after the opening date, and were a huge success. *BROADWAY MELODY* was held over for a second week, being followed by Al Jolson in *THE SINGING FOOL* and Hitchcock's *BLACKMAIL*. George Arliss, a big star of the thirties who lived at St. Margaret's Bay, was a frequent visitor to the PLAZA, recalls projectionist Gordon Bushell. The PLAZA, of course, made the most of this local celebrity's patronage in an advertisement which appeared in the DOVER EXPRESS on 8 August 1930.

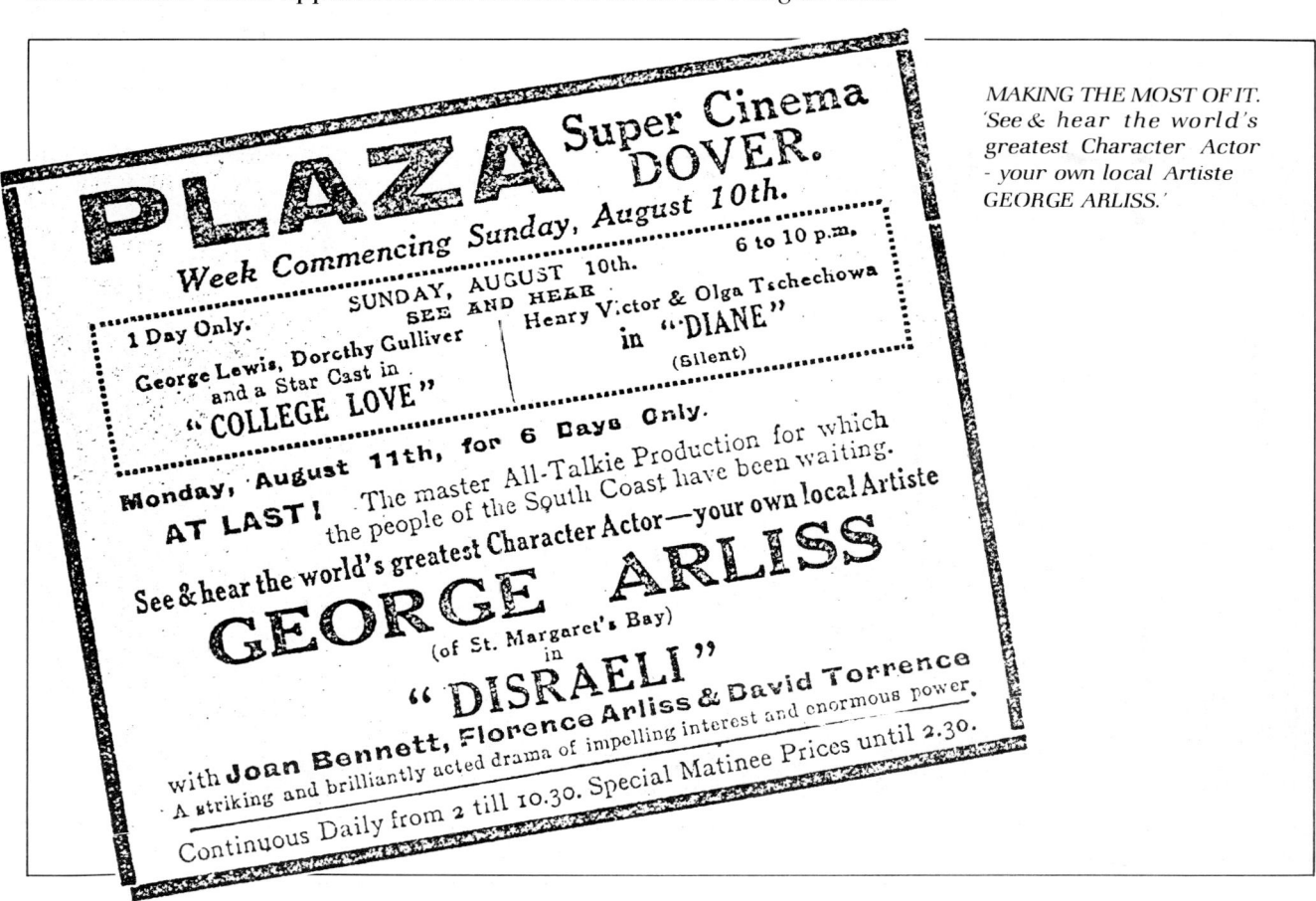

MAKING THE MOST OF IT. 'See & hear the world's greatest Character Actor - your own local Artiste GEORGE ARLISS.'

PLAZA Super Cinema DOVER.
Week Commencing Sunday, August 10th.

SUNDAY, AUGUST 10th. 6 to 10 p.m.
1 Day Only. SEE AND HEAR
George Lewis, Dorothy Gulliver and a Star Cast in "COLLEGE LOVE" | Henry Victor & Olga Tschechowa in "DIANE" (Silent)

Monday, August 11th, for 6 Days Only.
AT LAST! The master All-Talkie Production for which the people of the South Coast have been waiting.
See & hear the world's greatest Character Actor—your own local Artiste
GEORGE ARLISS
(of St. Margaret's Bay)
in "DISRAELI"
with Joan Bennett, Florence Arliss & David Torrence
A striking and brilliantly acted drama of impelling interest and enormous power.
Continuous Daily from 2 till 10.30. Special Matinee Prices until 2.30.

THE PLAZA threatened by fire. The cavernous entrance to the Metropole Building in Cannon Street, not only gave access to the PLAZA cinema but also to the Metropole Hotel, offices of the East Kent Poster Service and the Metropole flats. A fire in 1936 at the Hotel was therefore of much concern to the occupants of the various premises, but fortunately the fire was soon brought under control. The photograph (above) shows the over-the-pavement canopy bearing the cinema's name and a cut-price offer: "Full show at half price". This canopy played a vital part in the PLAZA's street publicity (see below). Note: Dover trams were still running in 1936.

CANOPY-TOP DISPLAY for the THE DAWN PATROL (1930) reflected the artistic talents of Dudley Pout, then of the East Kent Poster Service, who later became a famous commercial artist: see "Thanks for the Memories" in GRANADA section.

Although owned by a local syndicate (Messrs. Solly, Overs and Barnard), the PLAZA appears to have been managed by ABC from the beginning. Eventually the PLAZA became an ABC house with the ABC triangle appearing in press advertising in 1935, manager Sydney Sale of the GRANADA taking over responsibility for the PLAZA as well.

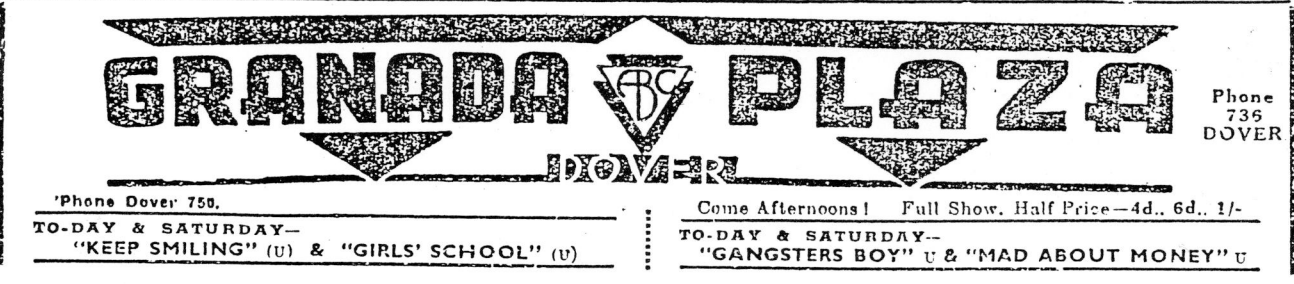

SIDE BY SIDE WITH ABC. This heading from a 1936 press advertisement emphasised that both cinemas were under the ABC banner.

The PLAZA was the scene of a brutal murder in July 1941 when the manager, fifty-year-old Richard Roberts was attacked with a fireman's axe, which was found near the body. The office safe had been opened and £30 was missing. Leslie Hammond, 18-year-old projectionist at the PLAZA was arrested, tried at the Old Bailey and sentenced to death. He was reprieved the day before he was due to hang and served a life sentence.

In April, 1951, the PLAZA passed into private hands, but the following year it was acquired by the Essoldo circuit. It was as the ESSOLDO that the cinema functioned until it closed in 1960. Later it became a Bingo hall.

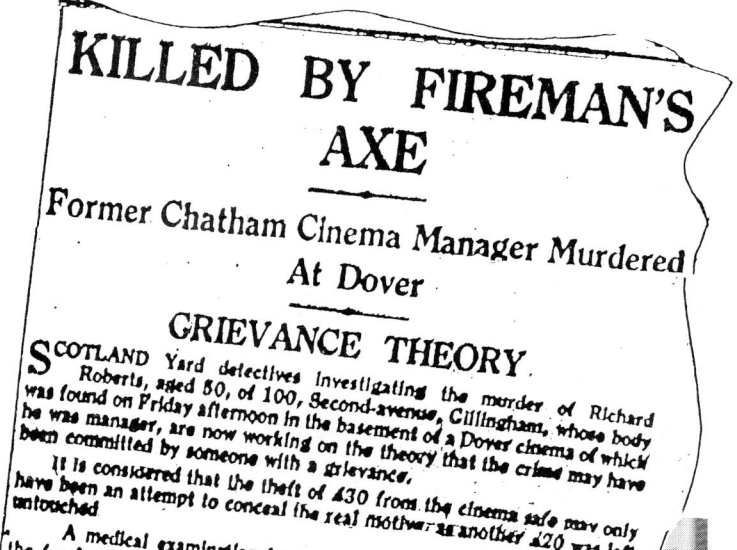

KILLED BY FIREMAN'S AXE

Former Chatham Cinema Manager Murdered At Dover

GRIEVANCE THEORY

SCOTLAND Yard detectives investigating the murder of Richard Roberts, aged 50, of 100, Second-avenue, Gillingham, whose body was found on Friday afternoon in the basement of a Dover cinema of which he was manager, are now working on the theory that the crime may have been committed by someone with a grievance.

It is considered that the theft of £30 from the cinema safe may only have been an attempt to conceal the real motive, as another £20 was left untouched.

A medical examination has revealed that deceased was struck on the forehead, and a bloodstained fireman's axe, which corresponds with the shape of the wounds, has been discovered by the police.

Roberts... manager of a Chatham

THE DOMINATING 'ESSOLDO' SIGN. The large, vertical sign which was erected when the PLAZA became the ESSOLDO, is clearly visible in this photograph of the 1958 Dover Carnival procession as it reaches Cannon Street.

Thanks for the Memories

Buckland Picture House/Regent

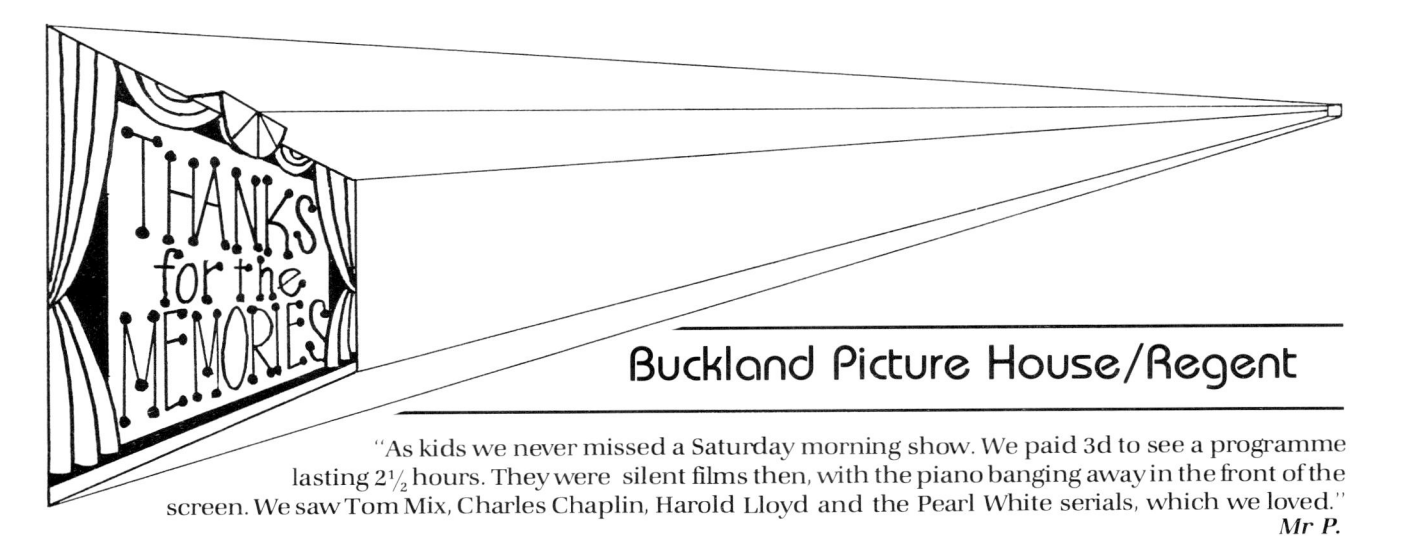

"As kids we never missed a Saturday morning show. We paid 3d to see a programme lasting 2½ hours. They were silent films then, with the piano banging away in the front of the screen. We saw Tom Mix, Charles Chaplin, Harold Lloyd and the Pearl White serials, which we loved."
Mr P.

"I remember seeing the Keystone Kops at the Buckland Picture House. I laughed so much that my mother had to put her hand over my mouth." *Mrs C.*

Charles Chaplin: Comic genius

Keystone Kops: Incompetent police

"The members of our cricket team made the cinema their Saturday night rendez-vous. After the show we used to vie with each other to walk the usherettes home." *Mr S.*

"I remember going to the cinema when I was a small child. A lady pianist played while the films were on. I loved Sunday nights because you saw the FU MANCHU serial; I used to be the first in the queue. When CHU CHIN CHOW was shown, the usherettes were all dressed up in Chinese costumes; it was magic." *Mrs S.*

Plaza/Essoldo

"The PLAZA did not open Saturday morning like other cinemas, but its kids' show was the first programme of the afternoon. You paid your 3d and when the juniors' show had ended, kept your head down until the first adult programme of the day began. I recall seeing a kids' show which included Laurel and Hardy's WAY OUT WEST, plus news, cartoons and a Three Stooges short, followed by CEILING ZERO from the main programme. Then there was an early-evening dash home, to be asked on arrival: 'What time do you call this then? I thought I told you to be home by such-and-such a time. If you can't do as you're told you won't be allowed to go again.....'." *Mr F.A.*

"I recall the murder there in July 1941. The stolen money was later found in the gent's loo near Charlton Green corn mill." *Mrs S.*

"On one visit a mouse ran up my husband's trouser leg, but fortunately it ran down again!" *Mrs B.*

"I have to own up that it was at the PLAZA I saw my first H-Certificate film. I looked over my shoulder to make sure nobody saw me going in or coming out of the cinema." *Mr A.*

INTERMISSION

Dover filmgoer Percy Collard was serving on RMS STRATHAIRD in 1932 and attended the "First Film Premiere Held on the High Seas". The cover of the souvenir programme shown here (reduced size) was in red, white and blue.

Souvenir of FIRST FILM PREMIERE HELD ON THE HIGH SEAS
Cruise to Norfolk Island Xmas, 1932

R.M.S. STRATHAIRD

Foreword.

THE Peninsular & Oriental Company and British Dominions Films take much pleasure in presenting to the passengers participating in the 1932 Christmas cruise to Norfolk Island, the first talkie premiere ever conducted in a British ship on the high seas.

These screenings mark the pinnacle of development that has been reached by two stellar British industries. Firstly, the growth of English shipping, as example, the structural magnificence and comfort combined in the "Strathaird," and their ability to render yet another entertainment service to patrons of their lines, that is, of course, the installation of talkies, and secondly, the strides forward that have been made by the production of British motion pictures, an example of which, also, will be demonstrated to you by the screenings you are cordially invited to attend.

To make the absolute presentation of these films totally British, it is an interesting feature to remind passengers that the equipment on which the talkie pictures are reproduced is "Raycophone", the all-Australian equipment.

~Programmes~

"JACK'S THE BOY" — Starring—
Jack Hulbert
Cicely Courtneidge
Winifred Shotter

"Day in June"
"Daily Dozens at the Zoo"
"Summit Seekers"

"THE FAITHFUL HEART" — Starring—
Herbert Marshall
Edna Best.

"London's Peace"
"River of Romance"
"Big Game Hunting"
"Phantoms"

"LORD BABS" — Starring—
Bobby Howes
Jean Colin

"The Message"
"Life of the Jackeroo"
"Sebastapol"

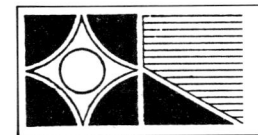

The Thirties

With the advent of talking pictures came the Super Cinemas, first seen in London and its suburbs, then in the provinces. Dover was one of the first provincial towns to be graced by one of these luxurious dream palaces: Sidney Bernstein's first GRANADA super cinema. When completed in 1930 it was acclaimed by the cinema industry as a great artistic success and its Russian-born designer was then commissioned by Bernstein to work on a chain of GRANADA cinemas, including the famous GRANADA, Tooting. Dovorians had never seen anything like this new cinema and flocked to enjoy the delights of films and live entertainment in luxurious surroundings. With such competition, attendances at the QUEEN'S HALL, WELLINGTON and the REGENT began to fall.

GRANADA LUXURY THEATRE

"A KING CAN HAVE NO MORE"

ILLUSTRATIONS from the Souvenir Programme, 8 January, 1930.

Granada
(later ABC), Castle Street

Granādā
(pronounced Gren-narr-dah)

The inspiration to create this luxury theatre was originally derived from the Alhambra Palace built eight hundred years ago by the Moors on the hills of Granada, Spain, where, undisturbed by the ravages of time, it still stands to-day—a monument of pride to the whole world.

How to pronounce it!

When, in the summer of 1929, preliminary work was started on the site chosen for Dover's first super cinema, it was discovered that a stream, part of the River Dour ran underneath it. Bovis, the main contractors, acting on the orders of architect Cecil Masey, arranged for huge stone blocks to be bedded into the river so that girders could be placed in position to keep the building clear of the water. Because of this and some other problems, the opening date had to be put back some six weeks. Recalls Mr W.T. Moore, who worked on the building: "The opening was fixed for the afternoon of Wednesday, 8 January, 1930, and as I was overseeing the marble work, I went in on the Monday, not emerging until the Wednesday, apart from a bite to eat. Sidney Bernstein and his wife were there, working for hours painting railings, assisted by Theodore Komisarjevsky, the designer. Throughout all that time, the stage acts and a troupe of dancing girls, together with Hedley Morton at the organ, and Leonardi's huge stage band of 20 musicians, were rehearsing. On the Wednesday afternoon the workmen left by the back door as the invited audience came in by the front door, with much of the paint still wet".

The Opening Ceremony was performed by the Mayor of Dover, Alderman Russell, and there followed the British Movietone News, a Mickey Mouse short, Hedley Morton's Organ Recital, the Pathe Pictorial, Leonardi and his Band with variety acts, the Granada Review and finally, *THE LAST OF MRS CHEYNEY*, starring Norma Shearer and Basil Rathbone. It could be truly said that the GRANADA had got off to a flying start, as queues on the succeeding days confirmed.

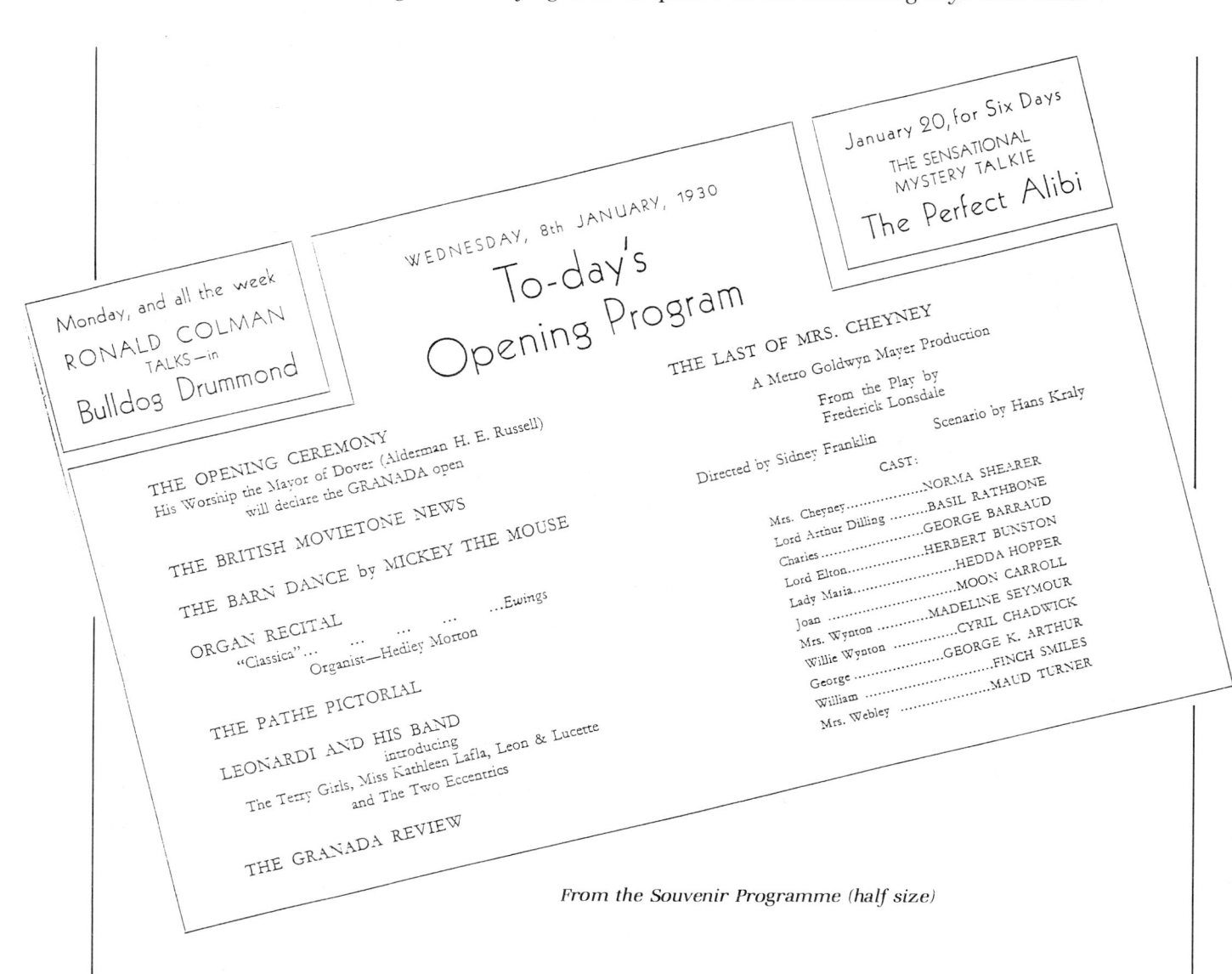

Monday, and all the week
RONALD COLMAN
TALKS—in
Bulldog Drummond

WEDNESDAY, 8th JANUARY, 1930
To-day's Opening Program

January 20, for Six Days
THE SENSATIONAL MYSTERY TALKIE
The Perfect Alibi

THE OPENING CEREMONY
His Worship the Mayor of Dover (Alderman H. E. Russell) will declare the GRANADA open

THE BRITISH MOVIETONE NEWS

THE BARN DANCE by MICKEY THE MOUSE

ORGAN RECITAL
"Classica"... ... ...Ewings
Organist—Hedley Morton

THE PATHE PICTORIAL

LEONARDI AND HIS BAND
introducing
The Terry Girls, Miss Kathleen Lafla, Leon & Lucette
and The Two Eccentrics

THE GRANADA REVIEW

THE LAST OF MRS. CHEYNEY
A Metro Goldwyn Mayer Production
From the Play by Frederick Lonsdale
Scenario by Hans Kraly
Directed by Sidney Franklin

CAST:
Mrs. Cheyney................NORMA SHEARER
Lord Arthur Dilling.........BASIL RATHBONE
Charles.....................GEORGE BARRAUD
Lord Elton..................HERBERT BUNSTON
Lady Maria..................HEDDA HOPPER
Joan........................MOON CARROLL
Mrs. Wynton.................MADELINE SEYMOUR
Willie Wynton...............CYRIL CHADWICK
George......................GEORGE K. ARTHUR
William.....................FINCH SMILES
Mrs. Webley.................MAUD TURNER

From the Souvenir Programme (half size)

SPARKLING IN THE SNOW. These two views of the GRANADA show the theatre at its best.

RONNIE RONALDE & ALL STAR COMPANY appeared there, week commencing 20 February, 1956.

SIDNEY BERNSTEIN has come a long way since he opened his first luxury cinema at Dover. He is now Lord Bernstein and in 1984 the British Film Institute awarded him a BFI Fellowship for his outstanding achievements in Film and Television.

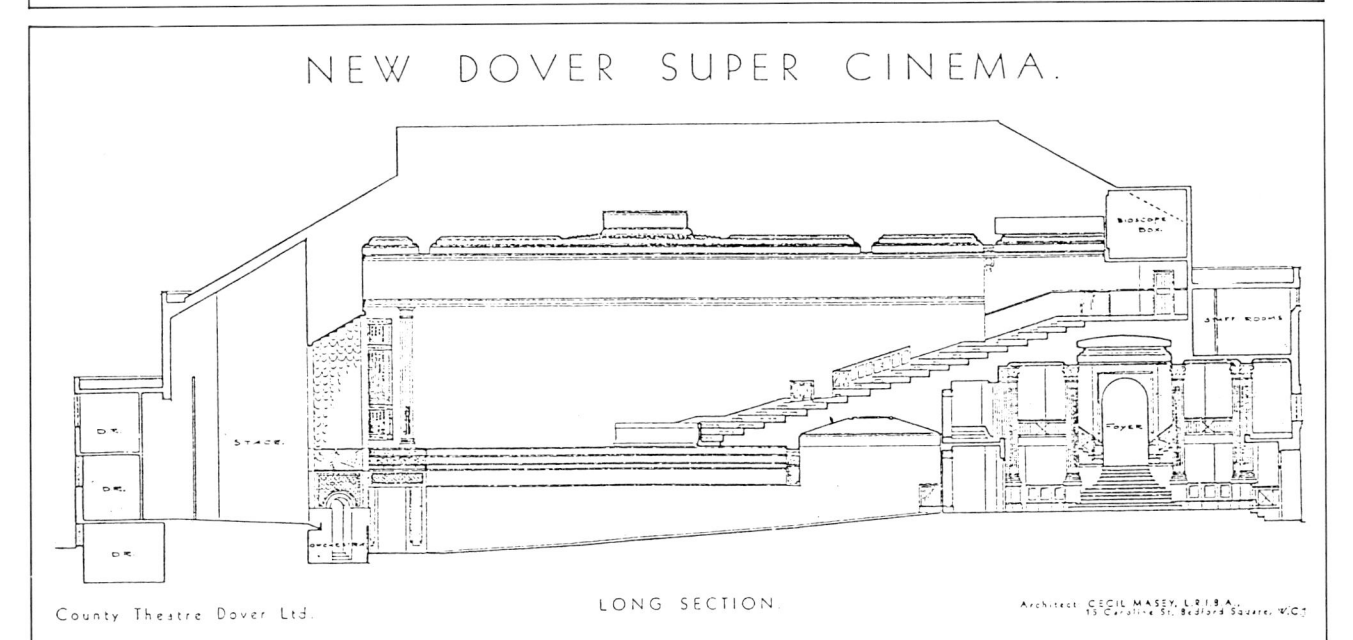

NEW DOVER SUPER CINEMA.

County Theatre Dover Ltd. LONG SECTION. Architect CECIL MASEY, L.R.I.B.A., 15 Caroline St, Bedford Square, W.C.1

BIOSCOPE BOX. An interesting aspect of this plan of the GRANADA, is the retention of the early-days name for what was generally known in the cinema world of 1929 as the projection box.

Externally, 'Dover's Wonder Cinema' was not unduly impressive, being a comparatively simple structure in the modern style using white stone and mottled brickwork, the main feature of the front elevation being a huge window. Internally, however, it was a different matter, for the building was decorated throughout in the Spanish-Moorish style by the Russian-born theatre and stage designer, Theodore Komisarjevsky, the second of whose three wives was Dame Peggy Ashcroft. Of the Dover GRANADA, Komisarjevsky said: "I succeeded in producing an effect of architectural harmony, of richness, and at the same time of restfulness". The up-and-coming Sidney Bernstein agreed, for he commissioned the Russian to apply his undoubted talents to a long line of Granada cinemas, most of them more magnificent than Granada No. 1.

Entry to the GRANADA was gained through two pairs of double doors beneath the canopy, leading to a marble-paved vestibule containing the pay boxes. Two more pairs of swing doors on the right gave access to the impressive foyer, also paved in marble.

The centrepiece was a grand marble staircase leading to an open balcony which encircled the foyer and provided access to the circle. Plain-papered walls accentuated the beauty of a series of scarlet-fluted columns with Corinthian capitols which were carried right up to the ceiling. Handsome Venetian mirrors adorned the walls, illumination being provided by one large crystal-glass pendant and a number of smaller units of a similar type. Whilst the foyer was perhaps the most magnificent part of the building, once inside the auditorium, patrons could not fail to be impressed by the Spanish-Moorish atmosphere created by Komisarjevsky.

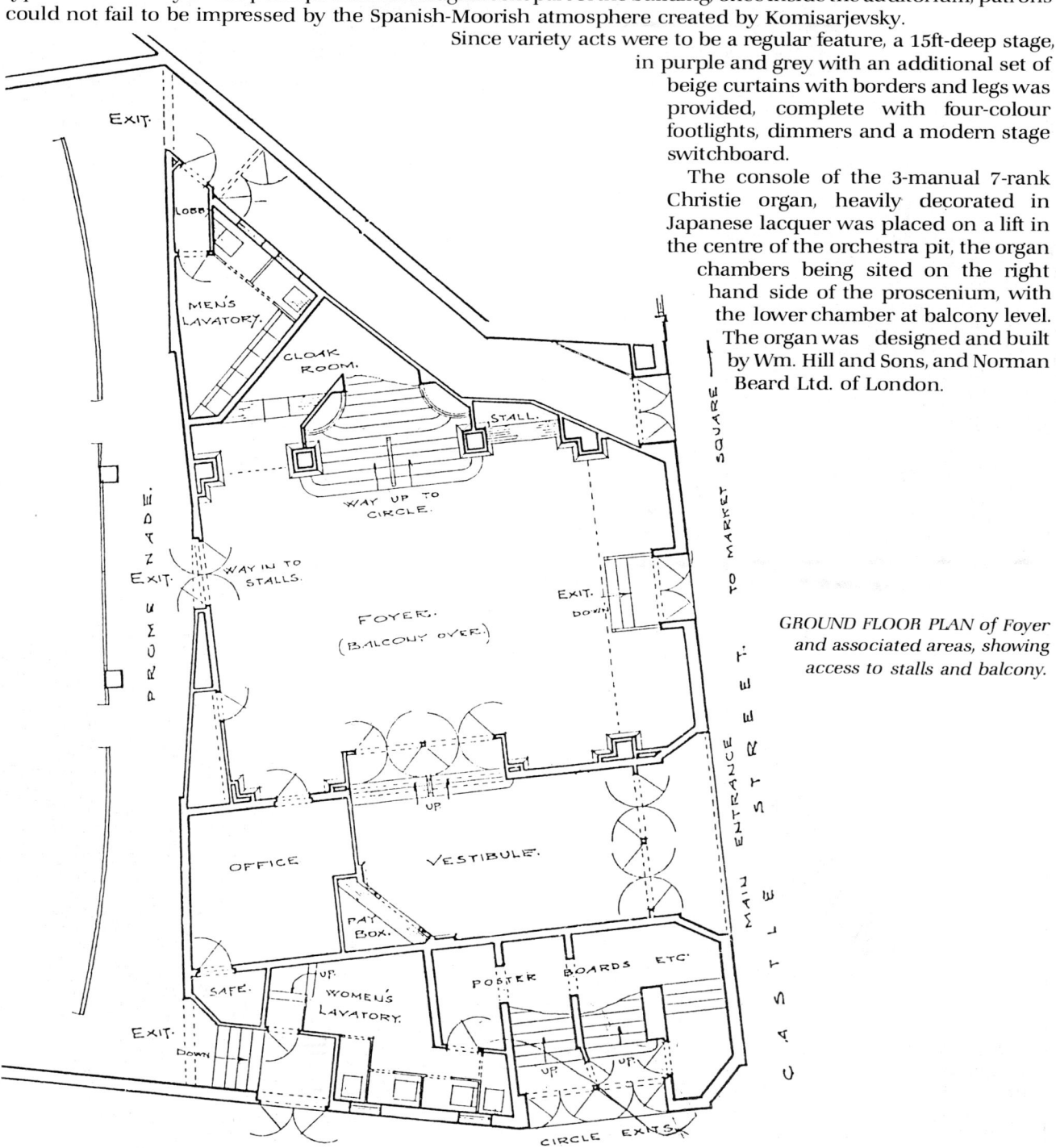

Since variety acts were to be a regular feature, a 15ft-deep stage, in purple and grey with an additional set of beige curtains with borders and legs was provided, complete with four-colour footlights, dimmers and a modern stage switchboard.

The console of the 3-manual 7-rank Christie organ, heavily decorated in Japanese lacquer was placed on a lift in the centre of the orchestra pit, the organ chambers being sited on the right hand side of the proscenium, with the lower chamber at balcony level. The organ was designed and built by Wm. Hill and Sons, and Norman Beard Ltd. of London.

GROUND FLOOR PLAN of Foyer and associated areas, showing access to stalls and balcony.

*THE GRANDEUR OF THE GRANADA
is captured by these poor-quality photographs
from a GRANADA advertisement in the Dover Official
Guide, 1930. Despite extensive research and enquiries of the
National Film Archive, Cinema Theatre Association and Lord Bernstein
himself, no other photographs of the auditorium can be found.*

STAIRCASE TO THE CIRCLE is shown in this photograph taken in October 1957, when Manager Sydney Sale retired. The mirror at the top of the photograph is reflecting the massive chandelier in the foyer.

WE ALL LOVE HIM! David Whitfield, surrounded by GRANADA staff during the week of 25 March, 1957, with the circle staircase again in the background.

The GRANADA, unlike the PLAZA, had taken full advantage of the talkie revolution, installing Western Electric sound equipment (both sound-on-disc and sound-on-film) along with modern Ross projectors. Ventilation of the theatre was by the Plenum system with 1500 cubic feet of either cooled or warmed clean air being provided hourly for every patron. Although a seating figure of 2,000 was quoted in publicity, the true figure was around 1,700 (stalls and circle). Seat prices were higher than other Dover cinemas (stalls 8d and 1/3d, circle 1/6d and 2/4d), but anyone with free time in the afternoon could enjoy a full show of a feature film, newsreel, variety acts and organ recital, for as little as 6d. Hours of opening were 2pm to 10.30pm on weekdays, 5pm to 9pm on Sundays.

Publicity played a big part in making known to Dovorians the name GRANADA. Long before the official opening, the local newspapers, poster sites and even the trams proclaimed: 'All roads lead to GRANADA.... Everybody will go to GRANADA.... SOON! GRANADA in Dover'. Guidance was also given in the pronounciation of the name: 'Say Gren-Narr-Dah' (in later years it became 'Gran-Ah-Dah'). And whilst the publicity department was busy promoting the theatre, the recruitment of high-quality staff by means of display advertisements in local newspapers was under way.

BUMPER PUBLICITY. The bumpers of Dover's trams were used regularly by the GRANADA to advertise the current film attraction. The photograph was taken during the week of 6 December, 1936, Len Easton being the driver, with Alf Rigden the conductor.

SPECIAL—ALL-TALKIE PROGRAMS—SUNDAYS

Sept. 7
"Sailors Holiday"
ALAN HALE

Sept. 14
"Big News"
ROBERT ARMSTRONG and CAROL LOMBARD

Sept. 21
"Paris Bound"
ANN HARDING

Sept. 28
"The Hottentot"
EDWARD EVERARD HORTON

PERFORMANCES COMMENCE AT 6 O'C. AND 8 O'C.   USUAL PRICES

SEPTEMBER

Harvest Time for Picture Fans

GRANADA

PHONE DOVER SIX AND BOOK YOUR SEAT

COVER OF POCKET PROGRAMME, SEPTEMBER 1929.
Inside were details of the weekday shows, including Harold Lloyd in WELCOME DANGER (8 Sept) and THE LOVE PARADE (29 Sept) with Maurice Chevalier and Jeannette MacDonald. All shows were supported by 'Leonardi and his boys' with 'Morton at the organ'.

ANOTHER GRANADA STAFF GROUP, 1958. Bidding farewell to "Dinks" the cashier after many years of faithful service to the cinema. Her husband was a projectionist at the GRANADA.

The recruitment of staff for the GRANADA was taken very seriously by the management, whose precise requirements were specified in the newspaper advertisements:-

> 'Male attendants age 30/35, height 5'6" to 6', chest 38" - Female attendants age 22/25, height 5'7" to 5'8", chest 32". Page Boys 14-16 years of age, 4'6" or less in height.'
>
> 'All staff must be intelligent, speak good English, be of very smart appearance and have good teeth. Previous theatre experience not essential. Application by letter only to GT, 197 Wardour Street, W1.'

Thorough training was given to all staff engaged, heavy emphasis being placed on courtesy and service. As for tips, patrons were advised:-

> 'SERVICE. Our staff is trained to give every courtesy. The offering of gratuities will be embarrassing both to them and you. In the interests of Granada service please advise the Manager of any inattention.'

What else did the GRANADA offer? A cloakroom, gratis, in the foyer. A car park at the special rate of 6d per car at the adjoining Dover Autocar Co. Ltd. Reserved seats for evening performances (no additional charge) which could be booked either at the theatre or at any of the offices of the East Kent Road Car Company at Canterbury, Folkestone, Deal, Sandwich and Cheriton - a wide catchment area.

Twelve months after the official opening on 8 January, 1930, no less than 982,750 people had visited the GRANADA. This first birthday, however, saw the disappearance of Leonardi and his Band together with Hedley Morton; not until 1934 did the stage shows (with Ernest G. Mitchell and his Band) and organ recitals (Sydney Amos at the console) make their re-appearance.

In July 1931, a new manager was appointed to the GRANADA. His name was Sydney Sale and before the first World War he had been a variety agent in London, where he knew many stars of the old music hall days. It was not surprising, therefore, that Sydney Sale was instrumental in bringing live entertainment to the GRANADA, besides drawing on his long experience as a cinema manager, the career he chose after his demob from the Royal Flying Corps in 1918.

MUSIC HALL STAR, NORMAN EVANS with Manager Sale in the foyer of the GRANADA, when he was appearing at the theatre week commencing 15 October, 1956.

Sydney Sale was the ideal cinema manager. Not only did he run the GRANADA with supreme efficiency and showmanship, but he had a strong sense of community spirit and the role of his cinema in Dover's life. As a fund-raiser for local charities, he had no equal, his patrons becoming ardent supporters of his many ingenious competitions and grand raffles. Thus, in 1932, when Sir Alan Cobham's Flying Circus came to Dover on National Aviation Day, GRANADA patrons were sold raffle tickets in aid of local charities, the prizes being flights over the channel in Cobham's planes. Looking through the local newspapers in those pre-war years, the name of Sydney Sale is seldom absent and his photograph regularly appeared with local celebrities and variety artistes appearing at the GRANADA. Amongst his hobbies was the collection of newsreel items featuring Dover, and it was these film clips which formed the basis of Ray Warner's first DOVER film.

When war came, Sydney Sale became an officer in the Home Guard, but despite his duties in that capacity and the shelling and bombing of the town, the GRANADA continued to provide entertainment and comfortable surroundings for the thousands of troops in the area. The KINEMATOGRAPH WEEKLY in January, 1943, praised Sydney Sale and two other Dover cinema managers (see below).

'Don't imagine for a moment', ran the article, 'that because of the conditions under which the GRANADA functions that it's a sorry-looking hall. Everything about it is spick and span - its cut-outs and vestibule displays are first-class, its sound is excellent, the usherettes neat, tidy and pleasant.'

These are the three Exhibitors in the front line at Dover. In the centre is SIDNEY SALE, Granada, exactly 19 nautical miles from the enemy and the nearest British kinema to Hitler. On the left is JOE ANTHONY, Regent, and on the right is S. M. BOND, Plaza. They, too, are in uniform, uniform of the Showman.

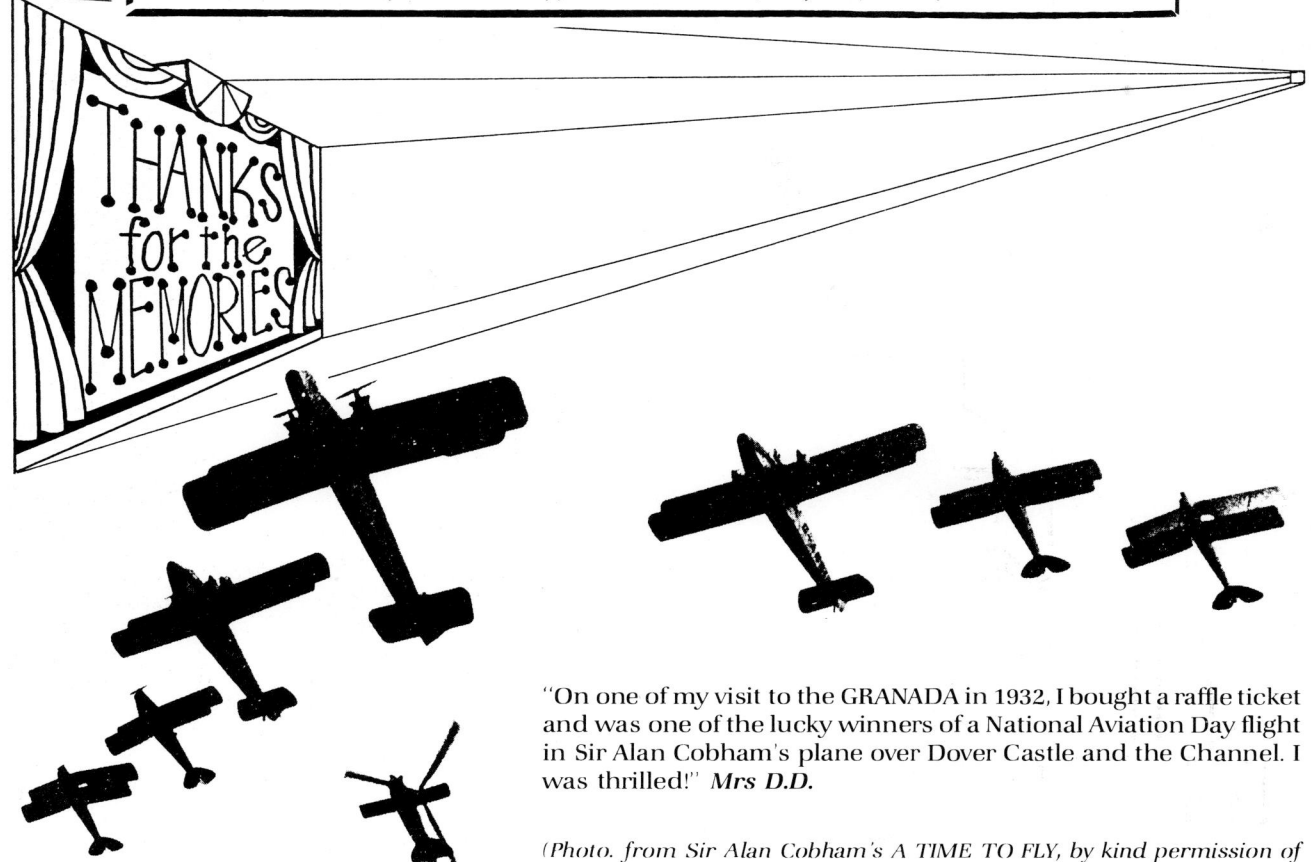

"On one of my visit to the GRANADA in 1932, I bought a raffle ticket and was one of the lucky winners of a National Aviation Day flight in Sir Alan Cobham's plane over Dover Castle and the Channel. I was thrilled!" *Mrs D.D.*

(Photo. from Sir Alan Cobham's A TIME TO FLY, by kind permission of Shepheard-Walwyn Ltd and Flight Refuelling Ltd.)

With peace, the GRANADA and Sydney Sale rapidly moved into top gear, a typical example of showmanship being the 1952 pre-release showing of a Battle of Britain film called *ANGELS ONE FIVE*, starring Jack Hawkins, Michael Denison and Veronica Hurst, the latter appearing in person outside the GRANADA:

> "Scenes of tremendous enthusiasm marked the appearance of Miss Hurst at Dover. Manager Sale had arranged for civic dignataries and high-ranking RAF personnel to receive Miss Hurst at the GRANADA, and had also arranged with the RAF for two flights of fighter aircraft to co-operate. The latter flew over the town in formation, and a pilot spoke over the intercom to the dense crowds around the P.A. Van in front of the theatre, frequently mentioning the title *ANGELS ONE FIVE*." (Kinematograph Weekly).

Small wonder that at the time of his retirement in 1957, Sydney Sale had been awarded more than a dozen certificates, special stars, citations of merit, an Honorary Life Membership of the Company of Showmen, and a 1956 award as the ABC Theatres' outstanding manager in Kent and Sussex, the GRANADA having been bought by the ABC chain in 1935.

Three years after Sydney Sale retired, the ABC-GRANADA (as it had been re-named) became plain ABC, and the Christie organ was removed for ultimate sale to a private organ enthusiast. Audiences began to decline steadily as people stayed at home to watch TV, and in the early seventies the GRANADA's circle seats were closed, leaving 610 seats in the stalls to cater for the remaining patrons. Finally, on 30 October 1982, the once-prestigious cinema ceased to function. At least Sydney Sale was spared the trauma of seeing his beloved cinema changed into a night-club: sadly he was killed in a car accident at the age of 78 while living with his daughter in Canada.

The ANGELS ONE FIVE promotion, 1952. The Mayor of Dover, John Fish, is standing between the two RAF officers on the left of the photograph, Sydney Sale on the far left.

JUST ANOTHER ABC. In 1960 the ABC-GRANADA became plain ABC, the Head Office decision which robbed the cinema of its identity.

BELOW. The DOVER EXPRESS story which says it all.

The last picture show

THE end of an era passed away unnoticed on Saturday.

Dover's last remaining cinema, The ABC in Castle Street, gave its final performance on Saturday night to a smattering of people then manager Mr Clive Batten shut the doors finally on what was one of the finest cinemas in the country.

Then he and his assistant manageress Mrs Hazel Ellis, chief projectionist of 14 years Mr David Robinson and the other staff picked up their coats and left.

It was a sad and disappointing goodbye to a cinema that had seen much better days.

Two people who did bid the ABC a fond farewell were cinemas' historian Mr Tony Thompson and Dover Film Society chairman Mr John Roy.

They wandered around the enormous building while Mr Thompson described how the country's first Granada cinema looked when it opened in 1930 amid great celebration and country-wide publicity.

The theatre seated 2,000, it was air conditioned and called Dover's new wonder cinema.

The local press plugged it with slogans such as "All roads lead to Granada" and "Soon! Granada in Dover."

Advertisements stated that those applying for jobs at the new cinema should "be intelligent, speak good English, have a very smart appearance and good teeth."

In those days the cinema offered a cloak room, telephones, a car park, monthly programmes and reserved seats. Seats then were 6d, 8d and 1/- to sit in the circle.

Fifty years later Dover's luxury theatre which set new standards of comfort and elegance has been unceremoniously axed.

At the grand opening in 1930 Mickey Mouse was the first film ever shown to a packed house, on Saturday The ABC ended with Pink Floyd — The Wall — shown to dozens of empty seats.

"It was a disappointing final evening. The numbers were very poor," said Mr Batten who begins a new job at an ABC in Bexleyheath.

Projectionist Mr Robinson is also being transferred to a cinema in Canterbury.

"The worst thing they ever did was to get rid of the circle seats. People enjoyed being able to pay more to sit in the circle and it was warmer too," he said.

Now the cinema is up for sale.

"It is sad it's closing but people just don't go to the cinema any more," said Mr Thompson.

EVERY picture tells a story ... and there will be no more pictures at the ABC. This was how the building looked this week.

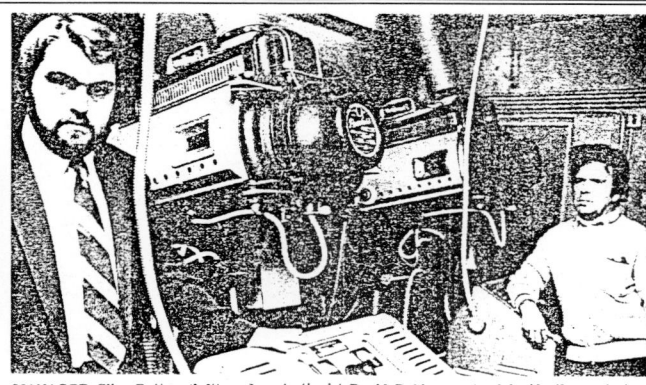

MANAGER Clive Batten (left) and projectionist David Robinson, stand beside the projectors that have been rolling since 1948, but were used for the last time on Saturday.

DOVER FILM SOCIETY tried to convince the owners that the cinema would flourish if converted to a 'Double' or a 'Triple', to provide a wider range of films and a more intimate atmosphere. Clearly, the cinema was too big. Alas, the battle was lost.

Thanks for the Memories

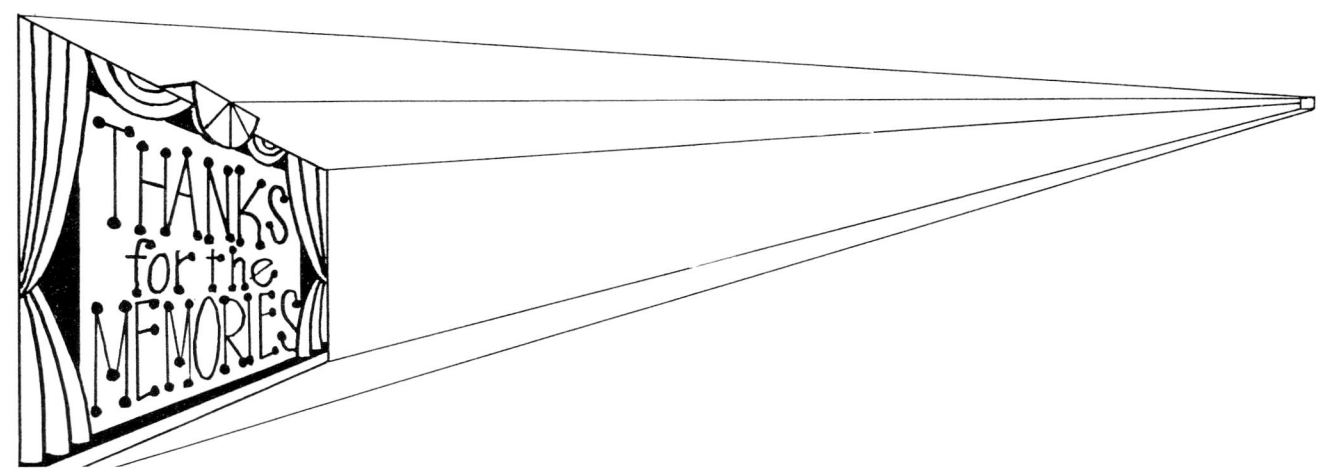

"A visit I made to the GRANADA, Dover, in 1930, was suddenly to change my occupation and, indeed, my way of life. On the front of the house were large hand-painted portraits of film stars, attractive displays in the foyer and panels with cut-out letters advertising the forthcoming attractions.

Here was art in an entirely new form. I think if the Principal of my art school had known that one of his past pupils was about to seek employment doing this rather low-grade work, he would have been shocked and disappointed.

It seemed a fortunate coincidence that the East Kent Poster Service in Dover, who were supplying all this new type of cinema advertising, needed another artist. I started the following week. This firm were also printing by silk screen which meant that small numbers of posters could be economically printed with designs and simple illustrations, making them more attractive than plain typeset posters.

An entirely new life had opened before me."

Dudley Pout

GRANADA front-of house cut-out display for PALMY DAYS (1932)

AUTHORS' NOTE. After two years with East Kent Poster Service, Dudley Pout became manager of the Stoll art studios at Chatham where he and five assistants produced cinema advertising, from press and posters to vestibule displays. Later he free-lanced in London, creating posters for many well-known films. He also moved into magazine illustration and for many years provided drawings for the famous 'Eagle' and 'Girl' childrens' magazines. The full story of his remarkable career can be found in THE LIFE AND ART OF ONE MAN OF KENT (Meresborough Books), and we are grateful to him for allowing us to print the above extract and illustrations from his book. See also PLAZA, Dover, and CENTRAL, Folkestone.

The new Regent
(later Odeon), London Road

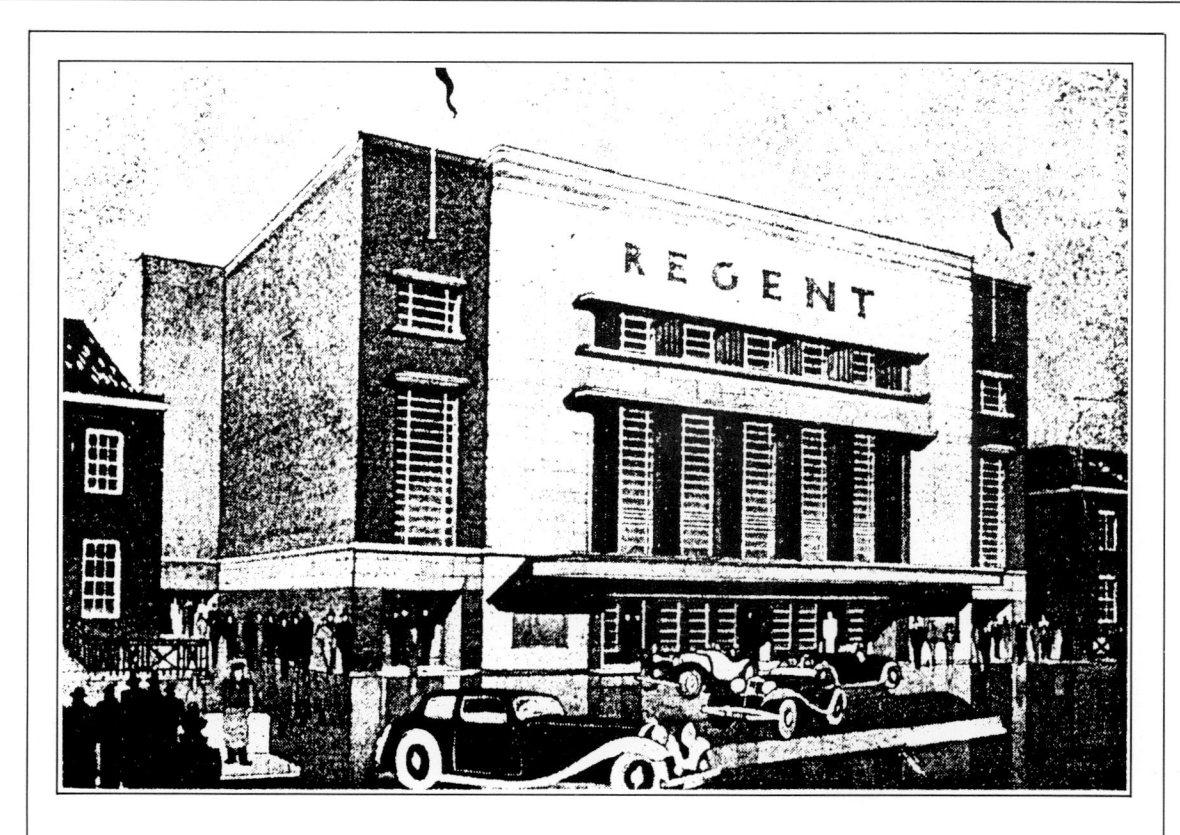

> This magnificent Theatre is designed on attractive and dignified lines. The architecture of the interior and scheme of decoration and furnishing adopted throughout the entire building imparts an atmosphere of warmth and welcome.
>
> *—From the SOUVENIR PROGRAMME, 27 March, 1937.*

When the old REGENT closed on 31 May, 1936, it seemed fitting that the last film shown was *THE IMPERFECT LADY*, starring Cicely Courtneidge. Would the new REGENT be the Perfect Lady? That was the question being asked by many of the loyal patrons of the familiar cinema then being demolished at great speed. They did not have to wait long to find out, for the new cinema opened less than a year later, surely a record for cinema construction.

'As in the old, so in the new REGENT: we will once again give you the best of entertainment....' announced Arthur Phillips, Managing Director of Universal Cinema Theatres Ltd., owners of the new cinema. 'The REGENT is a non-combine All-British Super Cinema', he went on. 'We are not bound by mass control or the routine of the large organisations'.

Certainly the opening of the new REGENT on 27 March 1937, by the Marquess of Willingdon, Lord Warden of the Cinque Ports, was one of the events of the year for Dover, while the choice of Will Hay, the well-loved comedian of radio and screen, as the guest of honour, ensured that every seat would be sold. There were also the attractions of *THE GREAT BARRIER*, starring Richard Arlen, the Technicolor cartoon *TOM THUMB* and a stage presentation by Hal Tauber and his Regent Orchestra. Hal Tauber, the special souvenir programme emphasised, had worked with orchestras at the Savoy, Claridges, Grosvenor House, the BBC and including the famous Tzigane Orchestra. The audience was suitably impressed.

The choice of manager for the new REGENT could not have been bettered. He was Basil Fortesque, for many years General Manager of the CENTRAL and PLAYHOUSE cinemas at Folkestone. Their loss was the REGENT's gain.

THE SOUVENIR BROCHURE for the opening of the new REGENT was an impressive production, measuring 11" x 9", and bound with ribbon. It reflected the importance of the occasion with no less a person than the Lord Warden of the Cinque Ports performing the opening ceremony. The Guest of Honour was WILL HAY, star of screen and radio.

WILL HAY's most famous film was OH, MR PORTER!

Souvenir Brochure of the Grand Gala Charity Performance on the occasion of the opening of the Regent Dover, by the Most Honourable The Marquess of Willingdon, G.C.S.I., G.C.M.G., G.C.I.E., G.B.E., P.C. Lord Warden of the Cinque Ports

Saturday, 27th March, 1937 at 8 p.m.

REGENT
GRAND GALA CHARITY OPENING PROGRAMME
SATURDAY, MARCH 27TH, AT 8 P.M.

1. **OPENING CEREMONY**
   By the Most Honourable
   THE MARQUESS OF WILLINGDON
   G.C.S.I., G.C.M.G., G.C.I.E., G.B.E., P.C.,
   (LORD WARDEN OF THE CINQUE PORTS)
   Supported by
   HIS WORSHIP THE MAYOR
   Alderman G. M. NORMAN, J.P.

   GUEST OF HONOUR,
   WILL HAY

2. **NATIONAL ANTHEM**

3. **"TOM THUMB"**
   CARTOON IN TECHNICOLOUR

4. **STAGE PRESENTATION**
   HAL TAUBER AND HIS REGENT ORCHESTRA

5. **REGENT NEWS**
   By arrangement with Gaumont-British

6. ## The Great Barrier
   Based on the 'Great Divide' by Alan Sullivan
   Featuring
   RICHARD ARLEN
   with
   LILLI PALMER

   THE PLAYERS

Hickey	RICHARD ARLEN
Steve	BARRY MACKAY
Moody	ROY EMERTON
Mary Moody	ANTOINETTE CELLIER
Lou	LILLI PALMER
Major Rogers	J. FARRELL MACDONALD
James H.	REGINALD BARLOW
Van Horne	ARTHUR LOFT
Joe	BEN WELDON
Bates	JOCK MACKAY
Bulldog Kelly	HENRY VICTOR
Magistrate	ERNEST SEFTON
Sir John MacDonald (Prime Minister of Canada)	FRANK McGLYNN, Sr.

45

OPENING WEEK. THE GREAT BARRIER was still being shown supplemented by SPORTING LOVE, to provide a double-feature programme.

SNOW WHITE AND THE SEVEN DWARFS, the Walt Disney classic, was very popular when it was screened at the REGENT in 1938. The colourful tableau over the entrance to the cinema is typical of the enterprise shown by managements to attract the public's attention. Manageress at the time was Jewel Sutton who now lives in Florida.

INTERIOR views of the REGENT which seated 1850 in stalls and balcony.

The new REGENT stood well back from the main London Road and was provided with an adequate car park. It was an imposing building of simple modern design in stone and black faience with deep windows rising above an illuminated canopy. The black and white front, above which the name REGENT appeared in a red and gold illuminated sign, was flanked by brickwork set back and containing matching windows. The cinema was airconditioned and seated 1850 in stalls and balcony; it was lit by concealed, reflected lighting. Western Electric Mirrophonic Sound, just on the market in 1937, had been installed and, whilst there was no organ, full stage facilities had been provided complete with dressing rooms for, like the GRANADA, it was intended that variety acts were to be part of the staple fare. A café was also provided and this proved to be very popular with the patrons. The cinema was designed by Percy A. Kelly and Kenneth M. Winch of Elgood and Hastie, with Robert Cromie as consultant architect.

FRONT COVER of typical REGENT pocket programme.

WEE WILLIE WINKIE starred SHIRLEY TEMPLE and was shown at the REGENT from Sunday 26 December, 1937, with a special Children's Matinee on New Year's Day. As part of the publicity campaign, a large coloured picture of Shirley Temple was circularised to houses in the area, the above exhortation appearing on the reverse side.

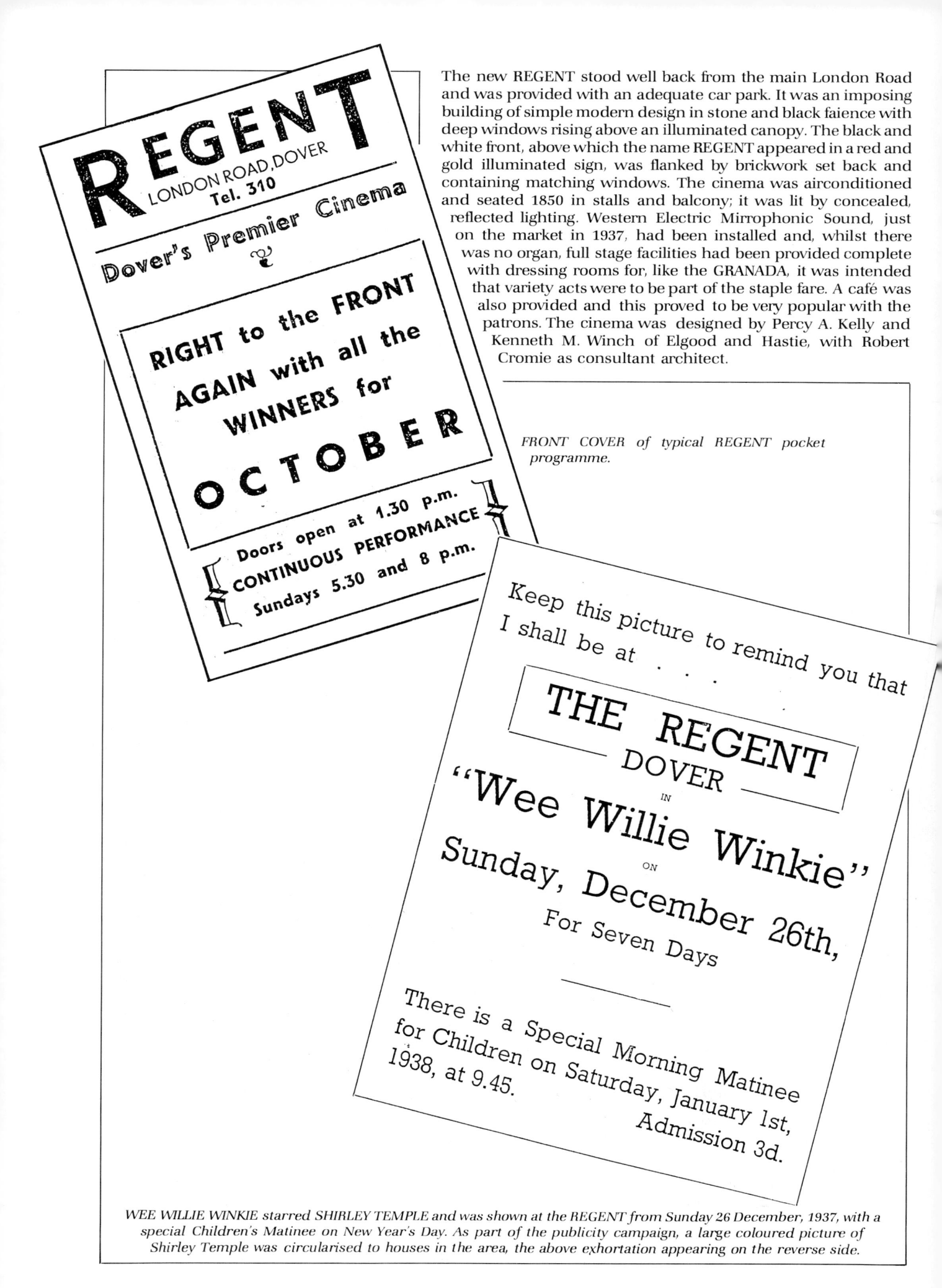

The REGENT enjoyed considerable success, thanks to good advertising and excellent management, not to mention the convenience of the car park alongside the cinema. When World War II came in 1939, the manager was Joe Anthony, who soon became well known to the many troops in and around Dover. If there was a power failure, Joe climbed on to the stage, lit the emergency candles held there in readiness and began to play the piano, singing at the top of his voice. Before long the REGENT would be ringing with the hundreds of voices singing the popular and patriotic songs of the time.

During the early war years, training films were shown in the mornings for members of H.M. Forces, particularly barrage balloon operators, with normal film programmes being screened in the afternoon and evenings. "They were hazardous times", recalls one of the projectionists. "I remember watching the Battle of Britain from the rooftop of the REGENT, with a Paramount News unit in the street below filming the battle."

In July 1943 the cinema was acquired by the ODEON circuit, although the name of REGENT was retained for some time. Eventually, however, the familiar ODEON appeared on the stone fascia and on the canopy. Faced with the competition from TV the ODEON audiences steadily declined until even the most faithful patron began to feel like a pea in a huge pod. Finally, closure came on 2 October, 1971, with *TOM JONES* as the last film to be shown. It was a sad day for the Manager and his staff of 20, who were then out of a job. Later the cinema was demolished to make way for a modern T.A. training headquarters.

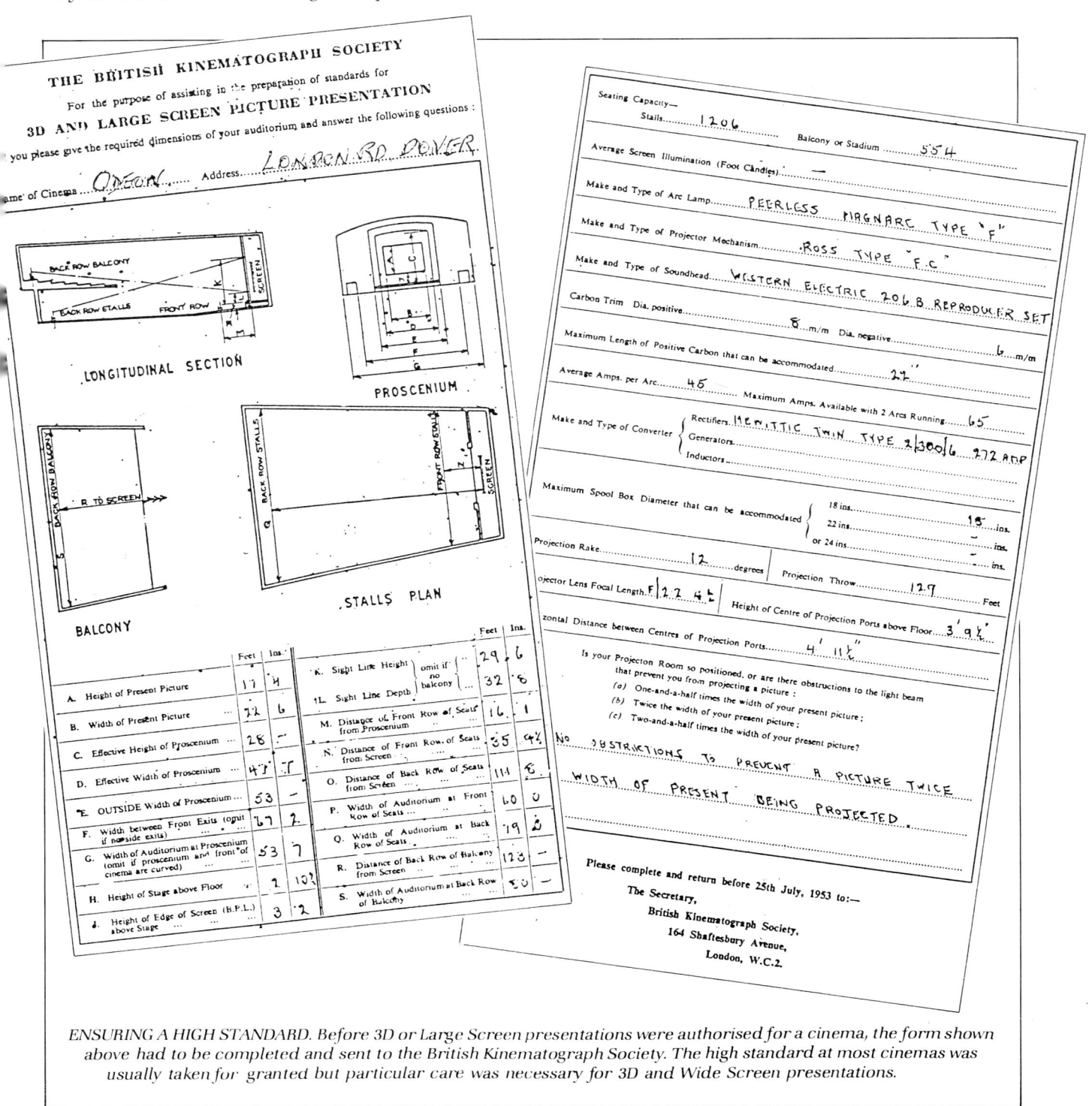

ENSURING A HIGH STANDARD. Before 3D or Large Screen presentations were authorised for a cinema, the form shown above had to be completed and sent to the British Kinematograph Society. The high standard at most cinemas was usually taken for granted but particular care was necessary for 3D and Wide Screen presentations.

TREASURE ISLAND
Wallace Beery, Jackie Cooper

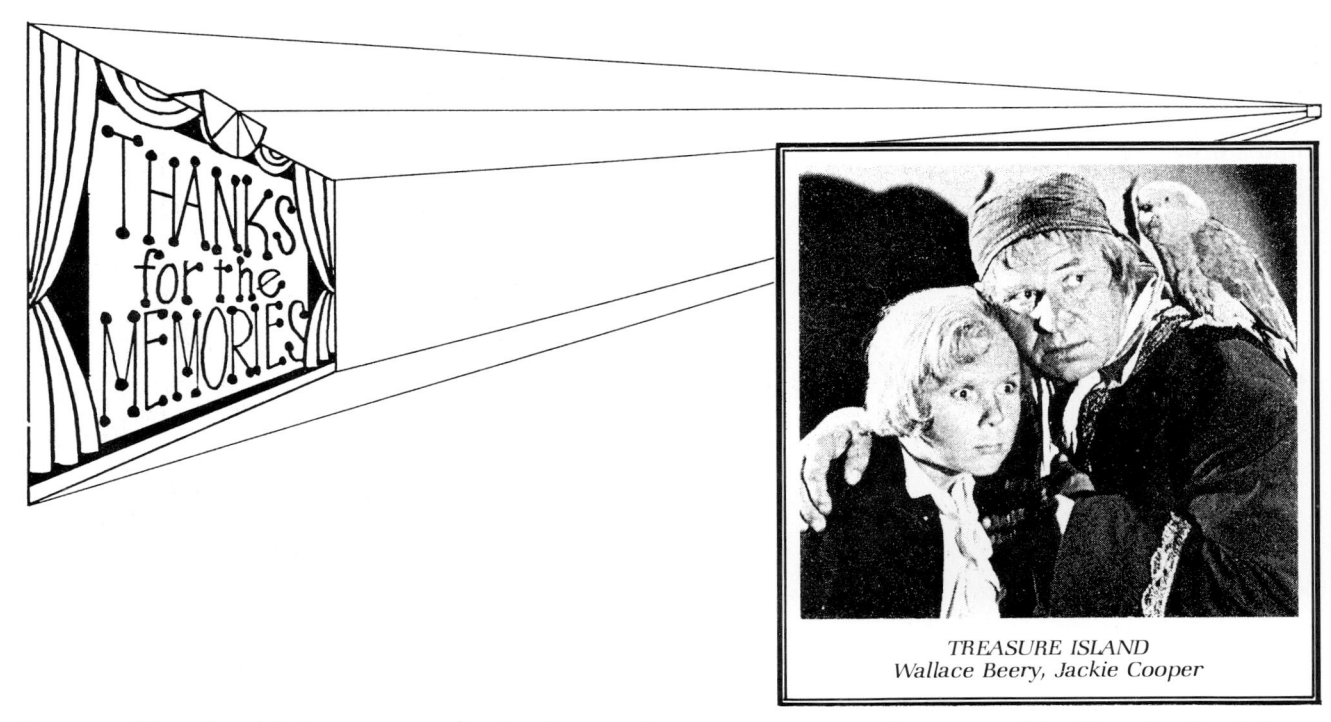

"To a small boy the old REGENT was a fascinating puzzlement. It was set on the terrace side of London Road above the level of the street, yet still needed a flight of steps to lead up to its entrance. There were internal surprises too. Access to the auditorium was gained through a door (or doors) at the side of the screen, so that you entered the dark from behind the screen in a state of disorientation.

The only films I can remember seeing there are the 1934 version of *TREASURE ISLAND* with Wallace Beery as Long John Silver, and Cukor's 1934 version of *DAVID COPPERFIELD*. I recall the latter because I sent myself to sleep for several nights afterwards by imagining all the terrible things I would do to that miserable Mr Murdstone, alias Basil Rathbone.

I remember the REGENT being demolished and the thousands of tons of chalk being removed to accommodate the new REGENT, much larger and more imposing than its predecessor. It kept the name REGENT until the early forties when it joined the ODEON circuit, a name ineluctably linked in my mind with the children's Saturday morning shows, admission three old pence. Handbills advertising them were pushed through letter-boxes in the area earlier in the week and prizes offered for half-a-dozen boys and girls who returned the cleanest to the cinema. The prize was sixpence. Presumably all the returned bills were used again the following week. Strangely, I retain nothing from those Saturday shows other than a few of the more improbable endings to some of the serials. From the main programmes, the newsreel of the HINDENBERG airship disaster sticks in my memory.

One morning, in 1937, the year of King George VI's coronation, all schoolkids in Dover were marched to the ODEON to see a 16mm colour film of a display in Crabble Athletic Ground earlier in the year. It was not until I saw the high-angle shots of the parades that I realised why some of us then had red uniforms, some white and the rest blue.

Finally I must mention the Manager for many years: Mr Anthony. He was one of the old breed of showmen who let his customers know who he was. He would speedily eject any loud-mouth who offended. And he was not shy of appearing on stage to extol the attractions of forthcoming programmes. On VJ day he enterprisingly arranged for Churchill's speech to be relayed over the cinema's speakers. What a pity that his kind are now a vanished species." *Mr F.A.*

THE UNFORGETTABLE NEWSREEL. In 1937, the Hindenburg caught fire upon landing at New Jersey with 35 lives lost.

Popperfoto

The REGENT becomes the ODEON.
When this photo was taken in the 1950s, the film being shown was DELIGHT starring Charles Chaplin.

RESCUED from the walls of an old garage being demolished in 1985, this late 1940s ODEON poster, still legible.

THE VESTIBULE OF THE ODEON was spacious and ideal for publicity displays, whether for films or community projects to which the cinema always gave support. The film FAST LADY was shown in 1962 (upper photograph) and the lower photograph features a display for MEALS ON WHEELS.

51

Thanks for the Memories

"Besides the joys of going to the Dover cinemas in my youth, there was also the hobby of collecting cigarette cards of film stars and swapping them with one's pals. I nagged my father into switching to 'Park Drive' cigarettes in the 1930s because of their 'Stars of Screen and Stage' series, which were particularly attractive because of their delicate colouring." *Mr C.*

Dover Today

THE KING'S HALL is now a popular Bingo Hall, but has retained its pleasant external appearance.

THE LUXURY GRANADA as a nightclub in 1986. Today the exterior has been painted over in cream and red (including the bricks) on conversion to a 'discotheque'.

THE PLAZA (ESSOLDO) became a Bingo Hall. The tessellated pavement at the entrance still reads PLAZA (upper photo) and the cinema's original display-cases are intact (lower photo) with the name ESSOLDO above.

THE QUEEN'S HALL and THE WELLINGTON HALL, pioneer picture palaces, have vanished without trace. Instead of the REGENT/ODEON there is a TA Drill Hall on the site. Only THE ROYAL HIPPODROME, where early animated pictures were shown, is commemorated by a plaque (see above) which is in Snargate Street.

PART TWO

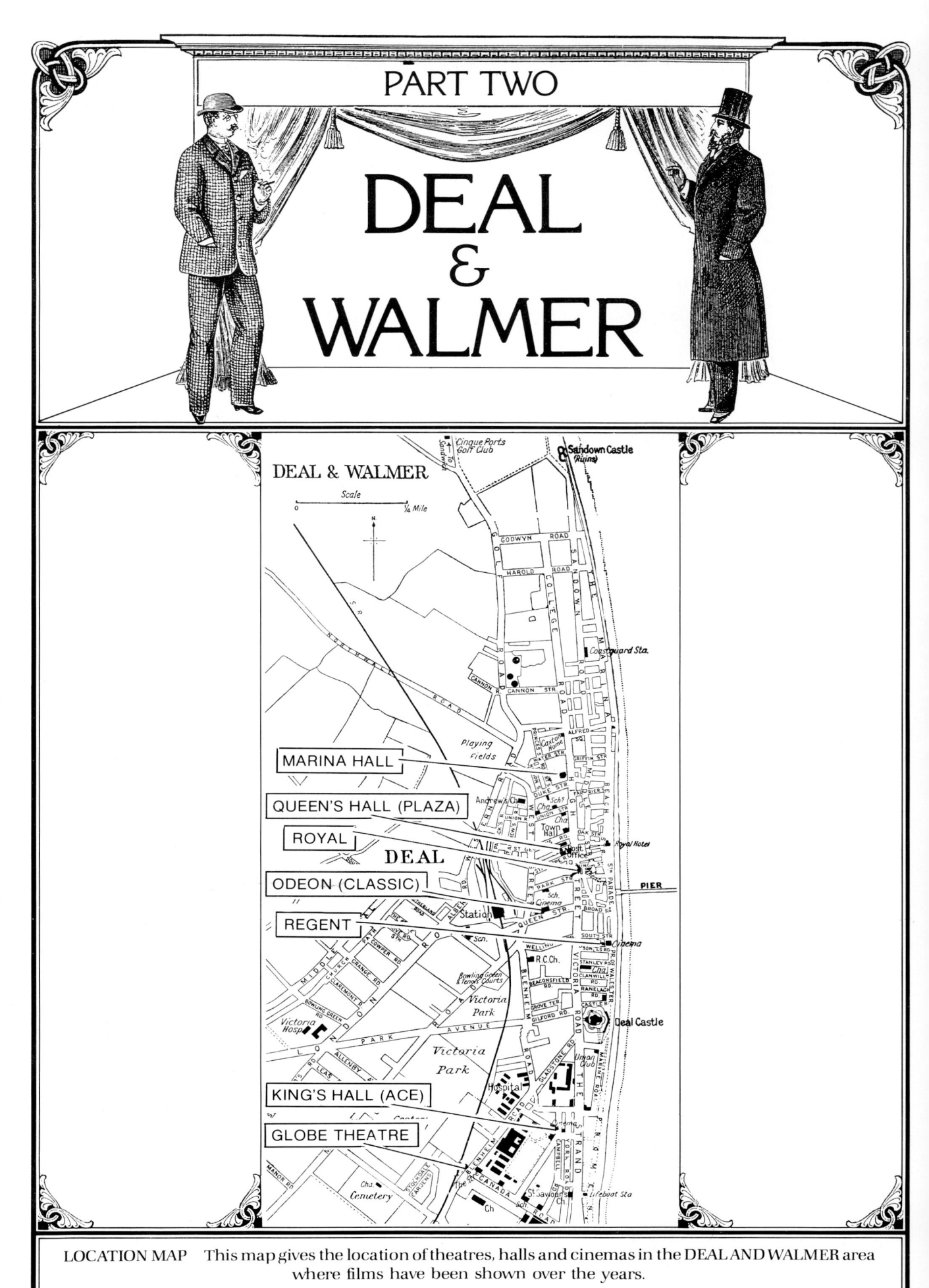

DEAL & WALMER

DEAL & WALMER

- MARINA HALL
- QUEEN'S HALL (PLAZA)
- ROYAL
- ODEON (CLASSIC)
- REGENT
- KING'S HALL (ACE)
- GLOBE THEATRE

LOCATION MAP   This map gives the location of theatres, halls and cinemas in the DEAL AND WALMER area where films have been shown over the years.
Based upon the Ordnance Survey map with the sanction of the Controller of H.M. Stationery Office.

Deal's first cinema
Marina Hall, High Street, Deal

Whilst it was the travelling showmen with their hand-cranked projectors who introduced the citizens of Deal to the exciting new world of animated pictures, credit for the establishment of a permanent cinema in the town must go to Charles W. Collins, a native of Ilford, who opened the MARINA HALL in 1910. Over the years, seven picture houses saw the light of day in Deal and Walmer and Charles Collins had an interest in at least four of them.

The MARINA HALL was originally the Assembly Rooms, a familiar feature of the High Street from as far back as 1795. According to Mr Collins, the Duke of Wellington and Lord Nelson had 'tripped the light fantastic upon the floor of the hall', but whether this was historically correct or not, many fashionable supper dances and balls were held there, and Officers of the Deal Battalion often put on theatrical events at the Assembly Rooms. By 1910, however, the property looked forlorn and neglected, so the offer by Charles Collins to transform the building into a Picture Hall was eagerly accepted.

The Grand Opening of the MARINA HALL took place on Monday, 11 April, 1910, with a programme of 'High-Class Up-to-date ANIMATED PICTURES'. The opening was very well attended and the following week the DEAL MERCURY reported: 'Mr Collins has very successfully adapted the Assembly Rooms to the purpose of a cinematograph show... the hall has been re-seated and provided with additional exits and with the apparatus contained in a fire-proof enclosure well away from the audience, so that due provision for safety is made... 90 minutes of entertainment at very popular prices'.

The success of the MARINA HALL was due not only to the attraction of the new medium of entertainment, but also to the superb showmanship of Charles W. Collins himself. He never neglected any opportunity to promote his cinema, using the local press, hand-bills, posters - and his own mouth, to secure maximum publicity.

THE FAMILY RESORT.
MARINA HALL,
HIGH STREET, DEAL,
(corner of Duke-street).
Grand Opening,
MONDAY NEXT,
APRIL 11TH,
With High-Class Up-to-date
ANIMATED PICTURES.
6.30.   TWICE NIGHTLY.   8.30.
Matinees: THURSDAYS & SATURDAYS, at 3.0 p.m.
Admission: Adults, 3d. and 6d. Children, 2d. and 3d.
Cycles, Mailcarts, and Perambulators stored free of charge.

GRAND OPENING advertisement in the DEAL MERCURY of 9 April, 1910.

When patrons arrived at the MARINA HALL, they were greeted personally by Mr Collins, who reminded them that they could park their cycles, prams and carts in the special area provided, entirely without charge. Then the Misses Sybil and Lizzie Collins, sitting snugly in their pay boxes, would also greet the customers, enquiring which seats they would like: 3d or 6d, but only 2d and 3d respectively for the children.

The other members of the extremely efficient back-up team were Charles Collins Junior (operating the Crossley gas engine which powered a dynamo to produce electricity for the projector and house lights); pianist Frank Pocklington who provided music for the silent films; Jack Baker an expert projectionist and, finally, two uniformed attendants who stood no nonsense from any unruly members of the audience.

THE MARINA HALL was featured in the KINEMATOGRAPH & LANTERN WEEKLY of 27 July, 1911. The ornate heading portrays Mr Collins (centre), Mr Baker (projectionist) and Mr Pocklington (right) the pianist. It was Mr Collins' view that 'a really first-class pianist is much more desirable than an orchestra.'

Programmes at the MARINA HALL usually lasted for about 90 minutes, with as many as ten films being screened, plus variety acts from time to time. The first film was usually a travel feature, so that late arrivals for the drama films did not have their enjoyment spoiled. Because few of the films carried titles, Charles Collins sometimes gave a running commentary, including the odd joke which always seemed to go down well with the audience of 300 sitting on their hard wooden seats. During the interval, in order to give Mr Pocklington a rest, music was supplied by a gramophone. At the end of the programme, Mr Collins appeared in person to express the hope that everybody had enjoyed the show. Then he would tell the audience about his next programme, which in his view should on no account be missed. Finally, there was a closing slide on the screen which showed a smiling Mr Collins and the words: MANY THANKS. GOOD-NIGHT.

INTERIOR of the MARINA HALL with its 300 wooden seats.

On Saturdays there were matinees for the children and these were very popular. Besides the films, the words of popular songs were put on the screen so that the children could sing them, accompanied on the piano by Mr Pocklington. There were no shows on Sundays as Mr Collins did not approve of Sunday entertainments, even had the authorities allowed it.

The entertainment activities of Mr Collins extended to the formation of a concert party in the summer of 1911, performances being given at the band stand and the Central Parade. Advertised as 'Mirth, Music and Magic' the show drew large crowds, the same audiences being invited by Mr Collins to join him at the MARINA HALL in the evening for a special showing of the Vivaphone film *THEY ALL LOVE JACK*.

Charles Collins' flair for showmanship was again demonstrated in May, 1911, when he bought a copy of the film showing the 'Death and Funeral of KING EDWARD VII, BY SPECIAL DESIRE AND REQUEST':

"This picture is the original, best and longest copy that was taken, being over 1,700 feet in length. It shows the procession leaving Westminster Hall, procession in London, Paddington, Slough, Windsor and at St. George's Chapel."

It is interesting to note that this same film footage is still included in archive material seen on TV, the projection speed having been slowed down by modern technology so that those portrayed in the film are seen at a normal walking rate.

The MARINA HALL appears to have closed down during the year 1913, for reasons which presumably were not unconnected with the many other entertainment interests of Mr Collins in the Deal and Walmer area.

ANNIVERSARY OF DEATH AND FUNERAL OF KING EDWARD VII. This was the film advertised in the DEAL MERCURY of 6 May, 1911, the astute Mr Collins being assured of full attendances because of strong local interest in the Royal Family.

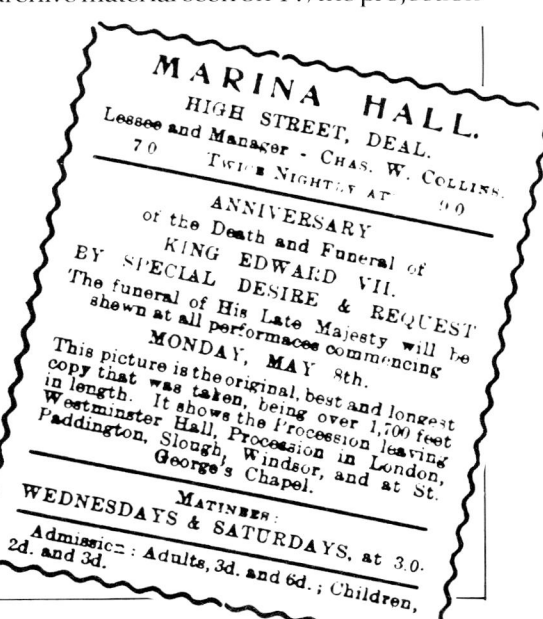

MARINA HALL.
HIGH STREET, DEAL.
Lessee and Manager - CHAS. W. COLLINS.
70 TWICE NIGHTLY AT 9 0

ANNIVERSARY
of the Death and Funeral of
KING EDWARD VII.
BY SPECIAL DESIRE & REQUEST

The funeral of His Late Majesty will be shewn at all performances commencing
MONDAY, MAY 8th.

This picture is the original, best and longest copy that was taken, being over 1,700 feet in length. It shows the Procession leaving Westminster Hall, Procession in London, Paddington, Slough, Windsor, and at St. George's Chapel.

MATINEES:
WEDNESDAYS & SATURDAYS, at 3.0.

Admission: Adults, 3d. and 6d.; Children, 2d. and 3d.

Globe Theatre
RM Depot, Walmer

When the Lords Commissioners of the Admiralty visited the Royal Marines Depot at Walmer on 18 May 1901, they made a point of inspecting the new GLOBE THEATRE, seating capacity 400, and expressed their approval. Little did they imagine that 9 years later, a certain Charles W. Collins would approach the Colonel Commandant and obtain his agreement to show Animated Pictures at the GLOBE THEATRE, "As shown at the Marina Hall, Deal". No doubt this new form of entertainment was greatly welcomed not only by the Marines but also by members of the public living locally, since they were thus spared the journey into Deal to visit the Marina Hall.

Over the years, films continued to be screened at the GLOBE THEATRE intermittently, interspersed with live shows and, at Christmas, the traditional pantomime with its Royal Marines cast. But it is no longer a theatre generally open to the public. This is a pity, because the theatre has a raked floor, tip-up seats, a balcony and a film projector which is still in place in the purpose-built projection room.

BY KIND PERMISSION OF THE COLONEL COMMANDANT. This DEAL MERCURY advert of 19 November, 1910, did not neglect protocol.

GLOBE THEATRE,
DEPOT ROYAL MARINES
(Entrance Canada-road).
Open for Public Performances of **Stage Plays**, in pursuance of the Army Act, 174a, 1889.
By permission of Colonel Commandant J. R. Johnstone, C.B., R.M.L.I.
THURSDAY, NOVEMBER 24th, 1910,
and Nightly until further Notice.
Two Hours' Exhibition of
COLLINS'
Royal Animated PICTURES,
As shown at the Marina Hall, Deal.
Matinees every Saturday at 2.30; doors open at 2. Admission: Adults, 3d., 6d., 9d., 1s; Children, 1d., 2d., and 3d.
Evening Performance. Doors open at 7; commence at 7.30
Admission: Orchestra stalls (numbered and reserved), 1s; pit stalls, 9d.; front pit, 6d.; back pit and gallery, 3d.
Children under 12 years of age, half-price to Orchestra Stalls and Pit Stalls only. Children in arms not admitted. No smoking allowed. No money returned. Plan of the Theatre can be seen and seats booked at Mr. F. W. Bushell's, The Strand, Walmer.
Box Office open daily from 3 to 5, and 8 to 10.

VIRTUALLY UNCHANGED TODAY. The external appearance of the GLOBE THEATRE has changed very little since 1910, when this photograph was taken. The theatre is seldom used for film shows, although a projector is still in place.

Queen's Hall
(later Plaza), High Street

The ubiquitous Charles Collins was not involved in this new cinema enterprise, the promotors being the Queen's Cinema Company of Ramsgate. It was in July 1912 that Arthur Sykes, manager of the QUEEN'S HALL PICTURE PALACE, challenged the competition with his advertisement in the DEAL MERCURY claiming that the cinema was 'The Finest, Most Comfortable and Best Ventilated Hall in Deal'. Certainly one of the attractions for patrons were the 305 plush tip-up seats in the cinema, a great improvement on the wooden chairs provided at the MARINA HALL.

Another attraction at the QUEEN'S HALL was the change of programmes on Mondays, Wednesdays and Fridays, thus catering for the addicts of the silver screen for whom once-a-week visits were not enough. And with prices at 3d and 6d ('Children Half-price to 6d seats'), the cinema did well, as waiting queues demonstrated.

In 1930 the cinema changed hands, the new lessees investing heavily in improved seating, a larger screen and the all-important sound apparatus to make it 'Deal's First Talking Picture Cinema' when it re-opened as THE PLAZA on 16 June, 1930. The 'Grand Opening Day' film was *HOLLYWOOD REVUE*, with a host of Hollywood stars, including Marion Davies, Norma Shearer, Joan Crawford and Buster Keaton. THE PLAZA was a popular Deal rendezvous for the next seven years, until competition from the ODEON proved too great. After closure, the building was converted into shops, but it is still recognisable as a one-time cinema.

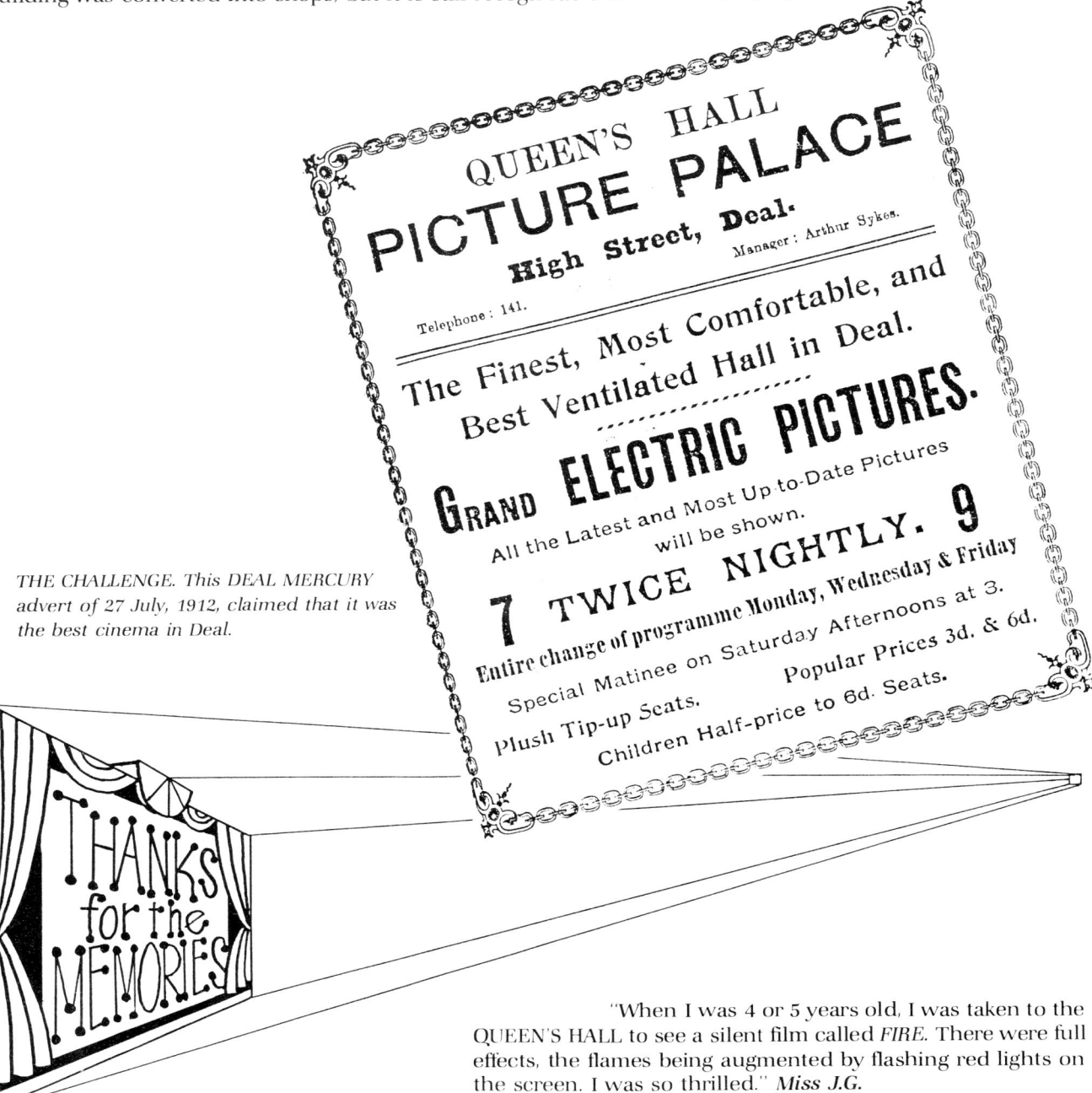

THE CHALLENGE. This DEAL MERCURY advert of 27 July, 1912, claimed that it was the best cinema in Deal.

QUEEN'S HALL PICTURE PALACE
High Street, Deal.
Telephone: 141.   Manager: Arthur Sykes.

The Finest, Most Comfortable, and Best Ventilated Hall in Deal.

Grand ELECTRIC PICTURES.
All the Latest and Most Up-to-Date Pictures will be shown.

7 TWICE NIGHTLY. 9

Entire change of programme Monday, Wednesday & Friday
Special Matinee on Saturday Afternoons at 3.
Popular Prices 3d. & 6d.
Plush Tip-up Seats.
Children Half-price to 6d. Seats.

"When I was 4 or 5 years old, I was taken to the QUEEN'S HALL to see a silent film called *FIRE*. There were full effects, the flames being augmented by flashing red lights on the screen. I was so thrilled." *Miss J.G.*

QUEEN'S HALL, December 1918. The films being shown were ANNIE LAURIE and ALL ABOARD.

THE PLAZA,
DEAL.

Grand OPENING DAY,
MONDAY NEXT, JUNE 16th.

SEE AND HEAR

HOLLYWOOD REVUE,
The First Musical Revue of the Screen.
With
Marion Davies, Norma Shearer, Joan Crawford,
John Gilbert, William Haines, Buster Keaton.

TALKING.   SINGING.   DANCING.

Admission - - 6d., 1/-, 1/6.
All Seats bookable without extra charge.

Matinees: Wednesday, Thursday, and Saturday.

Visit Deal's First Talking Picture Cinema.

BUSTER KEATON was a particular favourite of Deal filmgoers and they were delighted to see him in HOLLYWOOD REVUE, which opened on 16 June 1930 in 'Deal's First Talking Picture Cinema', THE PLAZA, previously known as the QUEEN'S HALL.

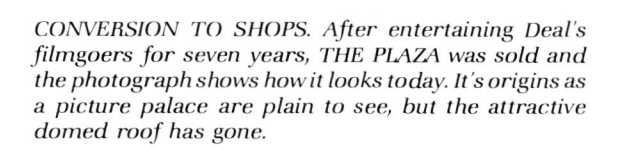

CONVERSION TO SHOPS. After entertaining Deal's filmgoers for seven years, THE PLAZA was sold and the photograph shows how it looks today. It's origins as a picture palace are plain to see, but the attractive domed roof has gone.

60

King's Hall
(later Ace, then Tivoli), North Barrack Road, Walmer

The architect for the KING'S HALL, which opened on 3 August, 1912, was a local man, C.L. Crowther, and the site chosen was originally occupied by the "Rising Sun" public house. The proprietors were Deal and Walmer Amusements Ltd, with Managing Director Chas. W. Collins ensuring that the films shown alternated with those at the MARINA HALL, his other major cinema interest.

The KING'S HALL was 64ft long and 36ft wide and could accommodate 344 people, segregated into three areas, rather like the 1st, 2nd and 3rd class passengers on the railways at that time. Each area was identified by a low rail with a hanging curtain. The best seats, upholstered in green velvet, consisted of a single row of 16 at the rear and were priced at 1/-d. The next block of seats (112 in all) were in crimson rexine and could be secured for 6d. The largest block, in green rexine, numbered 216 and were priced at 3d. To gain access to the cheapest seats, patrons had to walk to the far end of the hall by the screen and stage, where a stile and ticket office were installed. Performances were twice nightly at 7pm and 9pm, with matinees on Wednesday and Saturday at 3pm.

During World War II, the cinema was used in the mornings by the Royal Marines to show training films and just before the Dieppe Raid in 1942, when there were many Canadian forces in the area, two Canadian soldiers introduced themselves as projectionists by trade and were welcomed into the projection box where they happily took over. Mr Blanche of Walmer, who started as a re-wind boy at the KING'S HALL in 1943, recalls that if the curtains did not open to reveal the screen, it was his job to get a ladder, place it in position and try to open the curtains manually; this was while the film was running and with the audience shouting to him to get a move on. But Mr Blanche's chief memory was the esprit de corps at the KING'S HALL, with the male members of the staff seeing the usherettes safely home after the last performance, using dimmed torches in the black-out.

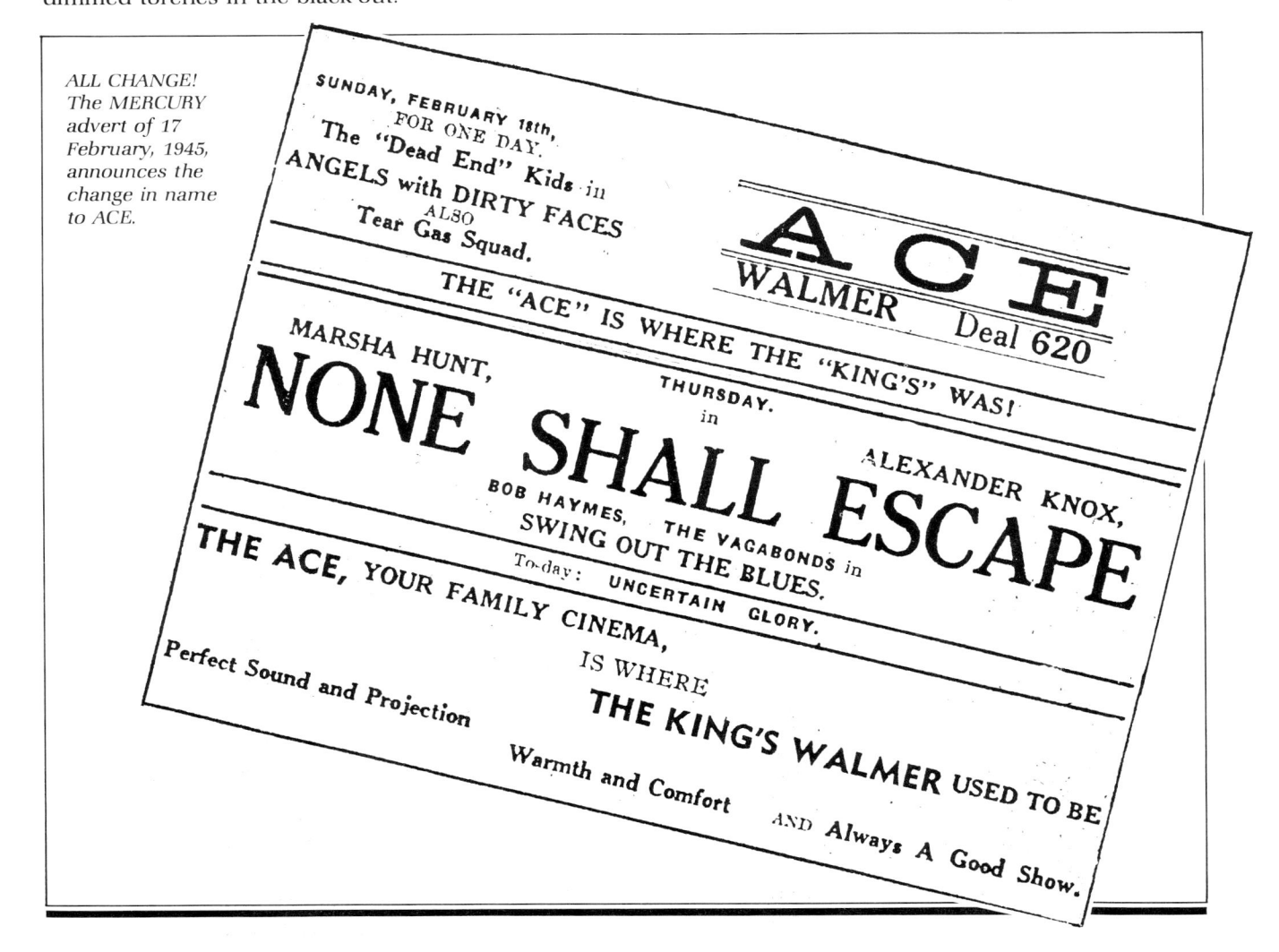

ANOTHER COLLINS ENTERPRISE. This KING'S HALL advert was in the DEAL MERCURY of 17 August, 1912.

KING'S HALL,
NORTH BARRACK ROAD, WALMER.

Proprietors
DEAL & WALMER AMUSEMENTS Ltd.
Managing Director...CHAS. W. COLLINS.

7.0.   Twice Nightly at   9.0.

COLLINS'
ROYAL ELECTRIC
PICTURES.

MATINEES—Wednesday & Saturday, at 3.

ADMISSION—Lounge 1s.; Second Seats, 6d.; Front Seats 3d.

ALL CHANGE! The MERCURY advert of 17 February, 1945, announces the change in name to ACE.

SUNDAY, FEBRUARY 18th, FOR ONE DAY.
The "Dead End" Kids in
ANGELS with DIRTY FACES
ALSO
Tear Gas Squad.

ACE WALMER Deal 620

THE "ACE" IS WHERE THE "KING'S" WAS!

MARSHA HUNT,
THURSDAY, in
NONE SHALL ESCAPE
ALEXANDER KNOX,
BOB HAYMES, THE VAGABONDS in
SWING OUT THE BLUES.
To-day: UNCERTAIN GLORY.

THE ACE, YOUR FAMILY CINEMA,
IS WHERE
THE KING'S WALMER USED TO BE
Perfect Sound and Projection
Warmth and Comfort
AND Always A Good Show.

The KING'S HALL played to packed houses throughout most of the war, with the AIR RAID WARNING slide on the screen being largely ignored by the mainly Forces audience. Only when the SHELL WARNING slide appeared did the patrons leave, usually with alacrity.

After the war, normal service was resumed, but in February 1945, the cinema was acquired by ACE cinemas, advertisements telling filmgoers: THE ACE, YOUR FAMILY CINEMA, is where THE KING'S, WALMER, USED TO BE. Subsequently the cinema changed hands again, being re-named THE TIVOLI. But despite these changes, which must have been bewildering to Walmer residents, audiences declined steadily and in 1949 the building was closed. It is now a garage and car showroom.

THE KING'S HALL building, as it is today, the old cinema providing ample accomodation for the garage and display area.

GONE WITH THE WIND

HANGMEN ALSO DIE

"I remember that in 1939 after the war had started, the ROYAL at Deal was due to show *GONE WITH THE WIND*, starring Clark Gable, Vivien Leigh and Leslie Howard. Then it was decided that a safer location would be the out-of-town KING'S HALL at Walmer. As I lived in Deal this was something of a nuisance, particularly in view of the black-out, but it was such a marvellous film that I went twice!" *Mrs R.A.*

"I used to see the silent serials *PEARL WHITE* and *TIN GUTS* at the KING'S HALL, loving every minute of it. Afterwards, we paid a visit to the nearby fish and chip shop; it was lit by oil lamps." *'Old Timer'*

"I think it was at the KING'S HALL, in about 1943, that I saw *HANGMEN ALSO DIE*, which was about the resistance movement in Czechoslovakia, when the hated Nazi named Heydrich was assassinated. It made me realise, young that I was, how a nation could be repressed and oppressed under a cruel occupation force, and it made a tremendous impression upon me and my schoolmates. Brian Donlevy was absolutely brilliant as the resistance leader: he should have recieved an OSCAR." *Mr K.R.*

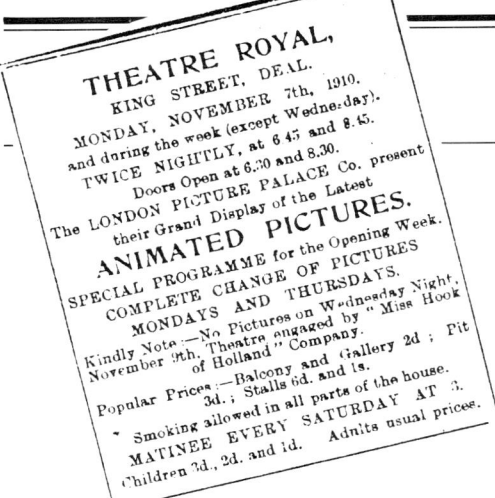

Theatre Royal
(later Royal Cinema), King Street

PACKAGE DEAL? It was the London Picture Palace Co. who presented the programme of Animated Pictures at the THEATRE ROYAL, as advertised in the DEAL MERCURY of 5 November, 1910.

This theatre started life as the Oddfellows Hall, the foundation stone being laid by the Mayor of Deal on 9 October, 1890. In 1892 it opened for plays, concerts and pantomimes, and in 1910 was given the more impressive name of THEATRE ROYAL. But as the DEAL MERCURY advertisement of 5 November, 1910, clearly shows, Animated Pictures soon became a feature of entertainments presented at the theatre. Destiny, in the shape of the redoubtable Charles Collins of Deal and Walmer Amusements Ltd., decreed that cinematograph projectors should be permanently installed, not to mention new tip-up seats for the audience of 600 or so, electric lighting and a new screen which ensured a picture-size of 18 feet in diameter.

On Monday, 19 May, 1913, the new order began with a programme which included a Travel Picture, BILLY'S BURGLARY, DURAND'S REVENGE (a Drama of Jealousy and Hate, 2000' of Film), BLOOD AND BOSH, MAUDIE'S ADVENTURE, and the GAUMONT GRAPHIC which included pictures of HMS New Zealand in South African waters, the Czar of Russia inspecting his Cossacks, and King Alfonso of Spain attending the march past in Paris of the Garde Republicaine. In addition, music for the silent films was provided by an orchestra directed by Herr Mendoza, late deputy conductor at the TIVOLI, Strand, London. Patrons paying 3d, 6d, or 1/-d for this cornucopia of entertainment, used the entrance in King Street, while those who could only afford the gallery (2d) or balcony (4d) had to use the side entrance in Middle Street.

In fairness to Charles Collins it must be said his selection of films demonstrated a keen eye for quality and in selecting the Italian-made epic QUO VADIS for screening in August, 1913, he could not be faulted. However, it may well be that showmanship had influenced his choice: five months previously QUO VADIS had been seen by King George V and Queen Mary at the Albert Hall, London, making King George the first British monarch ever to attend a public cinema.

WHITHER GOEST THOU? is the English translation of QUO VADIS, the answer for most Deal folk being 'To the Theatre Royal' to see this outstanding Italian film, shown in August, 1913.

"If you sat in the back seats at the ROYAL, you could hear the projectionists talking because the partitioning was so thin; the practice was to hammer on the partition with one's fist until they shut up." **Lt Col M.**

"In the days of the silent films at the ROYAL, you knew when the show was about to start because the pianist had a steel brace on his leg and you could hear him clanking his way down the aisle to the piano." **Mr N.**

"I was a projectionist at the ROYAL in 1958/9 and we used to have Horror Movie programmes starting at 11.30pm and lasting for two hours or more. There was a competition to see how many patrons could stay the course and we used a skeleton to add to the horror atmosphere. When we showed DR BLOOD'S COFFIN we had a real coffin in the foyer, with a dummy hand hanging from it!" **Mrs S.W.**

AN APPROPRIATE RE-OPENING FILM for THE ROYAL.
This advertisement appeared in the EAST KENT MERCURY on 10 February, 1934.

MOST POPULAR: GRACIE FIELDS

CHARLES LAUGHTON as HENRY VIII

The THEATRE ROYAL prospered over the years and in 1930 showed its first talking picture: *ALL QUIET ON THE WESTERN FRONT*. However, in July 1933 competition from the newly-opened REGENT cinema was felt and in November the theatre closed for modernisation. When it re-opened on 12 February 1934 with *THE PRIVATE LIFE OF HENRY VIII*, the cinema's name had been changed to THE ROYAL. Patrons loved the new surroundings: 'comfortable seats, luxurious decorations, gorgeous colour effects, perfect heating and ventilation', to quote the publicity at the time. Even old Mr Collins was pleased, though increasingly he was allowing his son to take the reins. But he still rode his bike round Deal, and Bill Nash, a re-wind boy at 13, recalls that he was paid 6d a week extra to clean the old chap's bicycle. During those happy pre-war days, the most popular films at the ROYAL were those of Gracie Fields. "People queued as far back as Barnards the Grocers", recalls a local resident. "And one day there was such a crush, the projectionist couldn't get into the cinema".

During World War II the cinema bore a charmed life, although Charles Collins was not so fortunate: his home was hit eight times. And immediately after Dunkirk, the ROYAL was the only cinema open in Deal. When peace came, business picked up and double-feature programmes were resumed, eventually under the banner of ASER Cinemas. But with the increasing popularity of television, attendances began to fall and in April 1981 the cinema closed. Early in 1982 the building was purchased by Mr and Mrs Woolls and turned into an entertainment centre with fruit machines and other electronic amusements.

STILL RECOGNISABLE. Despite its conversion to a Leisure Centre, the exterior of the ROYAL is largely untouched, with even the original display boards on either side of the entrance. The mock columns indicate its origins as a theatre.

Regent
Sea Front, Deal

It was in 1928 that the then Lord Warden of the Cinque Ports, Lord Beauchamp, officially opened the PAVILION THEATRE on Deal's seafront Victoria Parade, the Deal Council having committed itself to presenting good-quality shows there throughout the year. Unfortunately their efforts were not a commercial success and in 1933 the theatre was leased to two local business men, Jack Boyer and Harry Carey. In six short weeks and at a cost of around £7000, the PAVILION was transformed into the REGENT cinema, an achievement owing much to the ideas and enthusiasm of the architect, Percy Levett. The REGENT opened for business on 9 June, 1933, with a seating capacity of 911. Until the ODEON was built three years later, it was Deal's largest cinema, three times the size of the town's first picture palace, THE MARINA HALL.

THE PLEASING EXTERIOR OF THE REGENT. Although now used for Bingo, the exterior is virtually unchanged.

ROYAL
Sunday, July 1st, 7 days.

MOSS HART'S
WINGING ITS WAY TO THE SCREEN IN GALLANT ADVENTURE, LUSTY ROMANCE AND RINGING SONG!
WINGED VICTORY
Produced by DARRYL F. ZANUCK
Directed by GEORGE CUKOR
Presented by 20th CENTURY-FOX (U)

Sun., 4.15, 6.55 Mon. and Sat. 2.20 5.00, 7.40.
FULL SUPPORTING PROGRAMME.

REGENT
Sunday, July 1st, for 1 day.
Jack Oakie, George Murphy in RISE AND SHINE.
Jeannette MacDonald in LOTTERY BRIDE.

From the fearless pages of VICKI BAUM'S most daring story and other secret sources
WARNER'S
Hotel Berlin
FAYE EMERSON HELMUT DANTINE RAYMOND MASSEY
ANDREA KING PETER LORRE ALAN HALE GEO. COULOURIS
Directed by PETER GODFREY

2.50, 5.30, 8.20.
Also Leon Errol, Baby Sandy, Robert Paige in
MELODY LANE.
1.50, 4.35 7.20.

IN DOUBLE HARNESS. Changes in ownership and management in the cinema world were constantly occurring. In 1945 ASER CINEMAS were running both the ROYAL and the REGENT as this EAST KENT MERCURY advert of 30 June 1945 shows.

It is perhaps surprising that when war came in 1939, the REGENT, being so near to the sea, was not immediately closed, but the cinema remained open throughout the war, apart from days when enemy activity made it impossible to continue.

Billy Grant, Chief Operator from 1933 to 1946, recalls that early in the war the military arrived and said that the flagpole at the front of the cinema would have to come down, because a spotter-plane might report the building as a signal station and an attack would follow. Being young, Billy volunteered to shin up the pole to unhook the guy-ropes, and this he did to the cheers of the soldiers. Later, a powerful searchlight was placed on the roof, power being supplied by a Lister diesel dynamo installed near the Timeball building. Billy was in the cinema preparing for a show when the first shells fell on Deal, but he and his lady assistant decided to continue their preparations: "the show must go on". In fact, Billy had a ringside seat on the war. From a verandah at the front of the cinema he observed an American ship, laden with lorries, jeeps and other war material, receive a direct hit; it blazed for many hours and was finally towed into the north end of Deal where it smouldered for weeks afterwards.

On another occasion, Billy spotted a mine bobbing alongside the promenade, but fortunately it drifted away from the vicinity of the cinema, being later destroyed by gunfire. A few weeks later there was a mysterious fire at the back of the cinema, but it was not due to enemy action: a mouse had eaten through an electric cable causing a short circuit!

As to the most popular film shown at the REGENT during Billy's time there, he is in no doubt that it was *KING KONG!* Although made in 1933 it was given a repeat showing during the war and was thoroughly enjoyed by the many American, Canadian and British servicemen in the area.

After the war, the REGENT continued to do good business and in the mid-forties was acquired by ASER CINEMAS, who also took control of the ROYAL. But attendances began to decline in the 1950s, despite an injection of X-films, and the cinema was closed in 1963, re-opening later as a Bingo hall.

MOST POPULAR FILM at the REGENT was KING KONG with Fay Wray and Robert Armstrong.

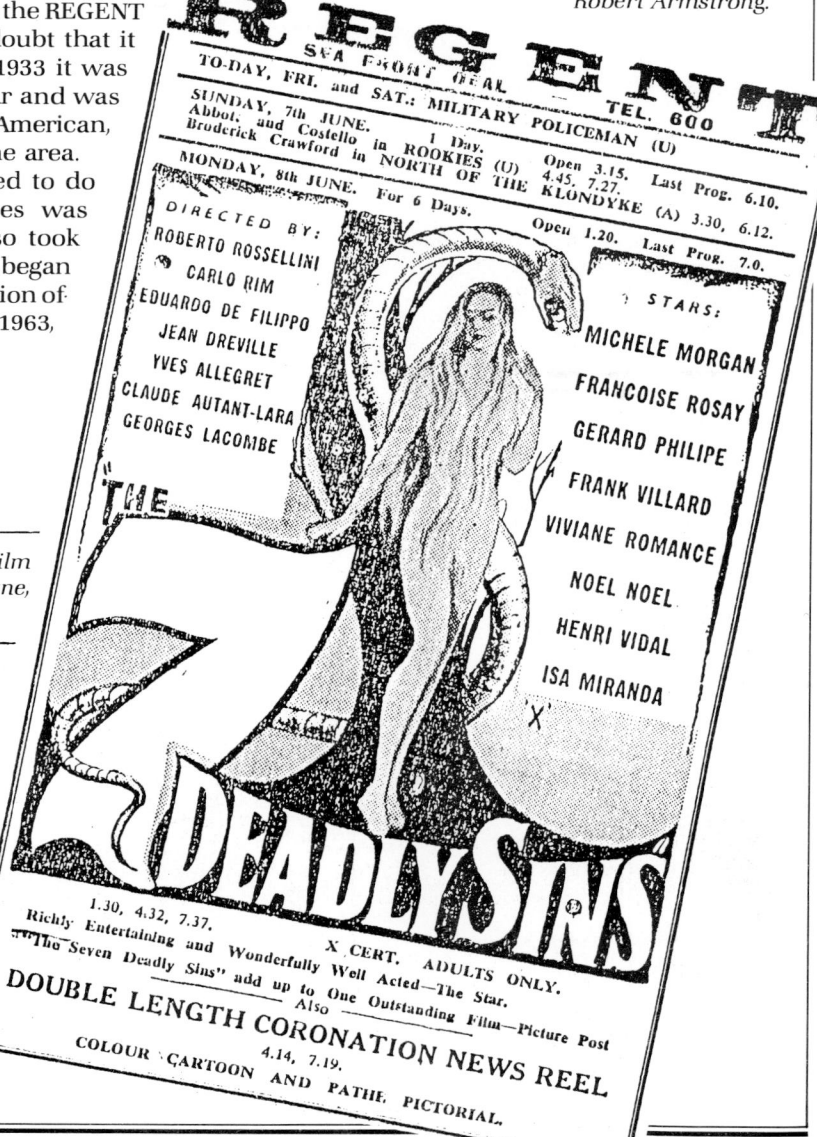

SOMETHING OF A CONTRAST: an X-film supported by the Coronation News Reel, 8 June, 1953.

Odeon
Queen Street, Deal

The driving force behind the ODEON chain of cinemas was the amazing Oscar Deutsch, son of Jewish immigrants from central Europe, whose empire grew from six cinemas in 1931 to 278 Odeons in 1941, the year of his untimely death at the age of 48. Of the 278 Odeons, no less than 140 had been specially built for his circuit, and the ODEON, Deal, was one of 35 Odeons opened in 1936. Oscar Deutsch's policy was not to spend a lot of money on elaborate interior decorations, nor to provide organ or stage facilities, since he was opposed to the films-plus-variety policy practised by many of his competitors. But as far as possible he sought to provide a distinctive exterior which would be clearly recognised as an ODEON.

The ODEON, Deal, was built on the site of the old Port Admiral's House, a gracious Georgian building which, in later years, had seen service as a school and private residence. The cinema's architect was Andrew Mather who, in 1936, designed nine other Odeons, including one at Faversham, of which the opening publicity blurb was equally true of the Deal cinema: "Every known means of art, science and hygiene have been introduced to further the comfort of patrons". No less a person than Mrs Oscar Deutsch herself, designed and supervised the interior decorations of the cinema, and this talented lady was present at the cinema's opening on 25 July, 1936, by the Mayor of Deal, Councillor J.G. Tooms. On that Saturday evening, all of the 932 seats in the stalls and circle were occupied, as were the 200 car parking spaces provided at the side of the cinema. It was a splendid occasion, many tributes being paid to all those involved in the provision of Deal's super cinema, "built by British labour with British materials and utilising a sound system made by British-Thomson-Houston Ltd." Even the star of the opening film, *MODERN TIMES*, was British-born: Charlie Chaplin.

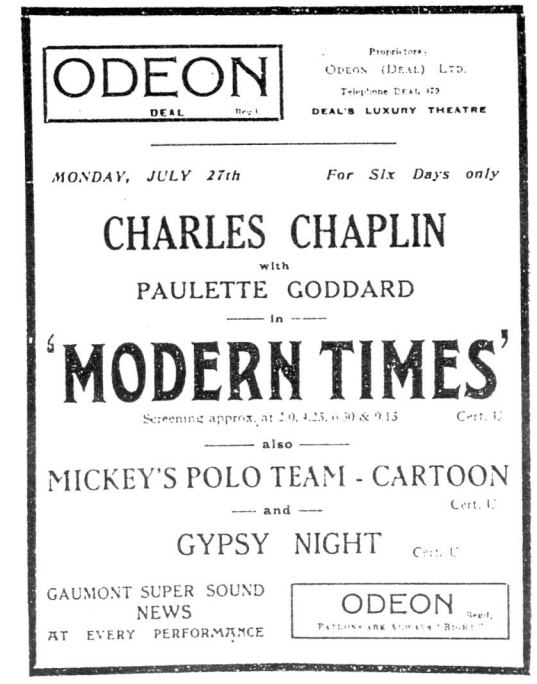

EAST KENT MERCURY, SATURDAY, JULY 25th, 1936.

FIRST WEEK OF OPENING. The sparkling new cinema brought joy to the filmgoers of Deal who queued to get in on 27 July, 1936, the film being MODERN TIMES with Charles Chaplin and Paulette Goddard. What a contrast to the photo taken on 31 January, 1984, see subsequent page.

INTERIOR of the ODEON

MODERN TIMES featured Chaplin working in a factory. This gave artist DUDLEY POUT the idea of using cog wheels as the motif for a poster.

The EAST KENT MERCURY of 1 August, 1936, provided a full description of the cinema for its readers. "The wide entrance doors open immediately upon a lobby containing the pay box, and from this leads a spacious entrance hall giving direct access to all parts of the house. The auditorium is planned on the new stadium system, and the screen can be plainly seen from every seat. All the gangways and seat spacings are ample and allow seats to be reached without discomfort or crowding, while great care has been taken with lighting and acoustics, every most modern device being used to give the utmost efficiency in these matters. The projection box, re-wind room, workshop etc., are all planned on ample lines and give the technical staff every opportunity of working with the utmost efficiency. There is in use the latest air purifying equipment which ensures a constant and steady supply of fresh, washed air, automatically maintained at an even temperature. Patrons inclined to deafness can use the B.T.H. deaf aids which are provided."

Years later, in 1980, David Atwell in his book CATHEDRALS OF THE MOVIES, was to list the ODEON, Deal, in his 'Gazetteer of Important Surviving Cinemas', a signal tribute.

THOSE HAPPY CHILDHOOD DAYS: ODEON Saturday Morning Cinema Club, 1937.

When war came in 1939, anti-aircraft guns were installed on the roof of the ODEON, but whilst they may have helped to keep raiding aircraft at a distance, the cinema suffered a bombing and machine gun attack in August 1942 which stripped the roof and caused other damage. The cinema was closed for several weeks for repairs, the manager ex-Grenadier Guardsman, Charles Bell, observing philosophically that there was probably more trouble on the way, which proved right.

Mr Blanche of Walmer went to the ODEON at the end of 1944 as a projectionist, when he was one of a team of nine, which allowed for days off and leave. He recalls how the doodle-bugs used to fly overhead towards the end of the war and the racket from the guns installed on Walmer Green as they tried to shoot the monstrous weapons down. But despite wartime conditions and supply problems, there was tremendous discipline in the projection box: all brass parts of the projectors had to be clean and polished, the manager inspecting them each day. Staff generally were also inspected daily to make sure they were properly dressed and well turned-out before the cinema opened.

Fortunately, the ODEON did survive the war, having provided comfort and cheer to the many thousands of allied troops who passed through Deal during the war years.

CARTOON FILMS were an essential part of the ODEON's Saturday Morning Cinema Club. Donald Duck was even more popular than Mickey Mouse.

FRIDAY, AUGUST 10th, 1951.

MR. WINSTON CHURCHILL TO RECEIVE FREEDOM

Full Details of Arrangements for Next Wednesday

11.55 a.m. Mr. Churchill will be escorted to the Odeon Theatre via the South and Victoria Parades, Deal Castle Road, Victoria Road, High Street and Queen Street.

The public are asked through the medium of the Press to decorate private and business premises with flags and suitable bunting along the route.

12 noon Outside the Odeon Theatre Mr. Churchill will inspect a Guard of Honour of Royal Marines.

In the foyer of the Odeon Theatre members of the Council, Freemen, the Mayoress, Mrs. Christmas Humphreys, Mrs. Daniels and Mr. John Arbuthnot, M.P., and Mrs. Arbuthnot will be assembled and introduced to Mr. Churchill.

Mr. Churchill with the Mayor, Aldermen and Freemen of the Borough will enter the auditorium and take their places on the dais.

The Ceremony will then open.

WINSTON CHURCHILL outside the ODEON after receiving the Freedom of the Borough of Deal. Under the cinema's canopy can be seen the 30ft-long poster reading: DEAL WELCOMES MR CHURCHILL.

When Winston Churchill came to Deal on 15 August, 1951, to receive the Freedom of the Borough of Deal, the ceremony was held in the ODEON cinema. Full details of the arrangements had been published five days previously in the EAST KENT MERCURY and it was clearly to be a great day for the ODEON, demonstrating the significant part cinemas played in the life of local communities, quite apart from showing films. Mr Bill Nash, projectionist at that time, recalls that Winston objected to the brightness of the spotlights as he stood on the stage and so they were switched off. But everything went well and Winston said he had thoroughly enjoyed his visit.

In 1967 the ODEON changed hands and was re-named the CLASSIC. Five years later, following the current trend, the cinema was closed while it was "twinned". When it re-opened on 30 June 1972 the two cinemas were advertised as CLASSIC ONE and CLASSIC TWO, each cinema seating 284. CLASSIC ONE tended to show the more important general releases, with CLASSIC TWO showing "X" films to a dwindling audience. Finally, on 31 January, 1984, the twin cinemas closed, much to the disgust of Deal and Walmer residents who now joined Dover as a cinema no-go area.

After standing empty for some time, the property was sold and became an entertainment centre with snooker and machines. But thanks to the enthusiasm of the ex-manager of the ROYAL cinema, Alexander Wallace, the 173-seat cinema named FLICKS was created from part of the old CLASSIC ONE. This small cinema is now prospering and was entered for the Cinema of the Year competition in 1987, the award going to the CARLTON, Westgate-on-sea, another non-circuit cinema run with enthusiasm by a management which cares for its patrons.

The CLASSIC cinemas close.....

.....but FLICKS CINEMA is created from part of the old CLASSIC 1

"I shall always remember the Coronation newsreel being shown at the Deal cinemas in June 1953. Because I am a staunch Royalist, I made a point of seeing the double-length newsreel by Pathé at both the ROYAL and the REGENT cinemas; I then went to the ODEON to see their special newsreel, made by Gaumont British News, I think. Then a fortnight later the ODEON showed *A QUEEN IS CROWNED*, which was in Technicolor and ran for over an hour. Incidentally, I do miss the newsreels when I go to the cinemas still left in Kent: they had a special quality which seems to be lacking in the news we see on TV." **Mrs J.J.**

This is the title frame of PATHE NEWS, one of the first British newsreels, which survived until February 1969. All the newsreels had their distinctive title frames: UNIVERSAL NEWS, GAUMONT BRITISH NEWS, BRITISH PARAMOUNT NEWS and BRITISH MOVIETIME NEWS, the last-named surviving the longest, its final issue being in May 1979 when it featured the 'Highlights of 50 years' and the Chelsea Flower Show.

"In the days of my youth I was a frequent customer of all the Deal cinemas and could not have enjoyed life without them. I also became an ardent reader of FILM WEEKLY until it merged with PICTUREGOER in 1939, becoming just PICTUREGOER after a few issues when the FILM WEEKLY title was quietly dumped. They used to pay guineas and half guineas for readers' letters and this was a useful source of pocket money for me. Then PICTUREGOER closed and I had to be content with copies of the ABC FILM REVIEW which I bought on my occasional visits to the ABC (originally GRANADA), Dover. However, that magazine really was "fan" fare and not a patch on the other two. My other film-related hobby was to collect cigarette cards featuring film stars and I still have some sets to this day." **Mr R.**

72

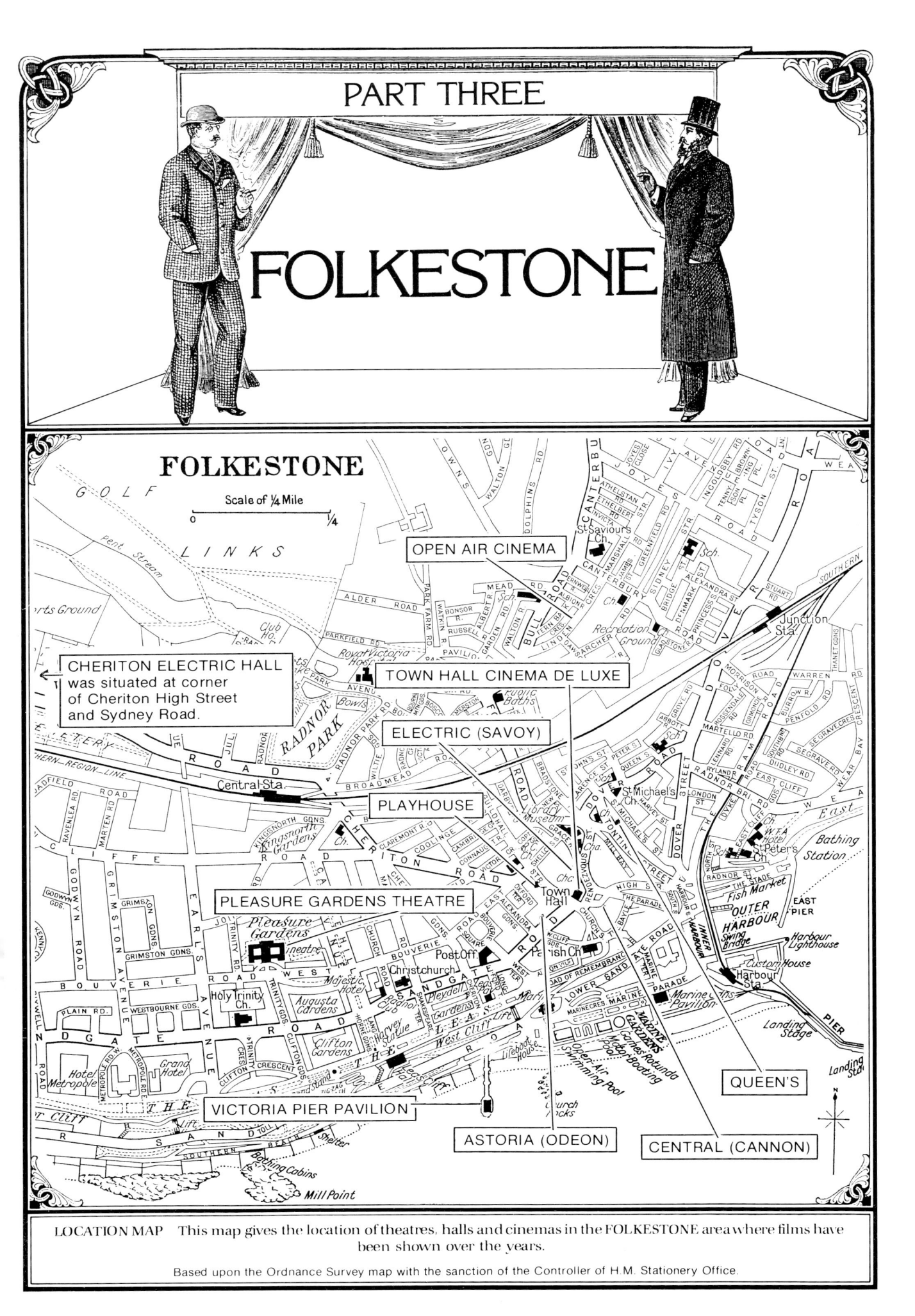

PART THREE
FOLKESTONE

FOLKESTONE
Scale of ¼ Mile

- OPEN AIR CINEMA
- CHERITON ELECTRIC HALL was situated at corner of Cheriton High Street and Sydney Road.
- TOWN HALL CINEMA DE LUXE
- ELECTRIC (SAVOY)
- PLAYHOUSE
- PLEASURE GARDENS THEATRE
- VICTORIA PIER PAVILION
- ASTORIA (ODEON)
- CENTRAL (CANNON)
- QUEEN'S

LOCATION MAP This map gives the location of theatres, halls and cinemas in the FOLKESTONE area where films have been shown over the years.

Based upon the Ordnance Survey map with the sanction of the Controller of H.M. Stationery Office.

73

Early Days

It was on 27 March 1897 that the FOLKESTONE HERALD published an advertisement about the presentation of POOLE'S GREATEST MYRIORAMA AND THE IMPORTANT ENGAGEMENT OF THE IMPROVED CINEMATOGRAPH at the PLEASURE GARDENS THEATRE for one week only.

The MYRIORAMA was a development of the Diorama, which used large translucent paintings to produce special effects with shutters and illumination. The enterprising Joseph Poole commissioned a team of artists to produce a series of scenes on a canvas about a mile in length and fifteen feet in depth, to 'glide past the spectator with an almost imperceptible motion entirely free from noise or friction'. A trained operator controlled the 'wonderful changes', including the illuminations which produced the special effects. The programme featured the ARTISTIC REPRODUCTIONS OF NATURE'S WONDERLAND, the CRETAN REBELLION, MATABELE WAR, JAMESON'S DASH INTO THE TRANSVAAL and THE MASSACRE OF THE ARMENIAN CHRISTIANS, all accompanied by a commentary and music by a small orchestra

As to the IMPROVED CINEMATOGRAPH, this was undoubtedly the improved version of the Theatrograph, a film projector produced by the London instrument maker, Robert W. Paul, a machine much sought after by travelling showmen to provide film shows in empty shops, church halls, music halls and marquees.

Although many people in Folkestone thought that animated pictures were but a passing fad, over the years film shows were given at a number of venues in the town, notably at the TOWN HALL CINEMA DE LUXE and the VICTORIA PIER PAVILION. These shows continued for several years, even after the first permanent picture palace was established in 1910.

Joseph Poole's brochure for the MYRIORAMA (Kodak Museum)

Robert W. Paul's Theatrograph No. 2 patented in 1896. (Projected Picture Trust).

These advertisements for Animated Pictures at the VICTORIA PIER PAVILION and for the TOWN HALL, CINEMA DE LUXE, appeared in the FOLKESTONE HERALD on 8th June, 1912.

VICTORIA PIER PAVILION
FOLKESTONE.

SUNDAY AFTERNOON AND EVENING.
Special Programme of
ANIMATED PICTURES.

MONDAY, JUNE 10th, AT 5 AND 8,
Entire change of Programme, including
"THE LIE" (War Drama).
WEDNESDAY EVENING,
BLADDER FIGHT ON THE OPEN-AIR RINK.
Also Gents' Singing Competition in the Pavilion.

THE VICTORIA PIER was opened in 1888 and the Pavilion seated about 1000. The Pavilion was destroyed by fire in 1945 and the pier was demolished in 1954.

TOWN HALL, FOLKESTONE.

OWING to the Election and other engagements, the
TOWN HALL CINEMA DE LUXE
will be CLOSED from
MONDAY, JUNE 3rd till WEDNESDAY,
JUNE 12th, 1912.

Pleasure Gardens Theatre
Bouverie Road West

The National Art Treasures building was erected in 1886 and with its glass roof and elaborate facade looked rather like the Crystal Palace. It was lit by electricity and a special railway line was built to it from Shorncliffe Station. In 1888, after conversion, it was opened as the Exhibition Palace Theatre, later becoming the PLEASURE GARDENS THEATRE with a seating capacity of 1500. Entertainment of every description, including the occasional cinematograph show (see previous page) was provided, and in 1913 the foyer was enlarged to make an impressive concert hall. Many of the great names in the entertainment world of the day, appeared at the PLEASURE GARDENS THEATRE.

In October 1956, the theatre was closed for structural alterations, including the removal of the pillars and the lowering of the ceiling in the foyer/concert hall, reputedly the coldest spot in town. New seating, a new heating system and the latest film projection equipment were installed.

The theatre opened as a cinema on 2 November, 1956, and struggled for some years with a diet of sub-titled films from the continent. But the experiment was not a success and it ceased to be a cinema in May 1964. Following a short spell as a 'Social Club', the building was demolished. Offices now stand on the site.

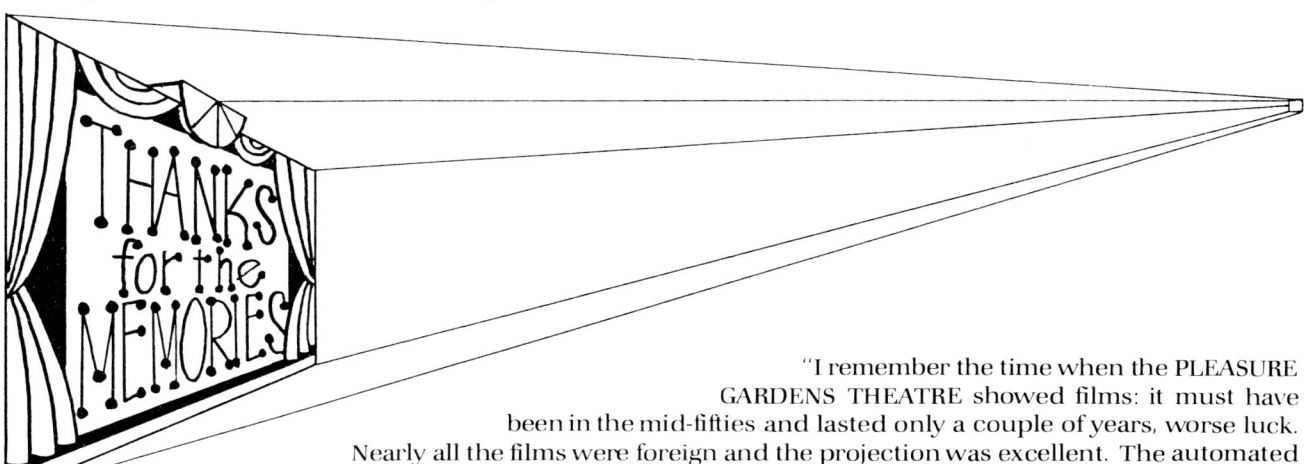

"I remember the time when the PLEASURE GARDENS THEATRE showed films: it must have been in the mid-fifties and lasted only a couple of years, worse luck. Nearly all the films were foreign and the projection was excellent. The automated equipment cost around £20,000 I was told. Whenever I went to see a film there the place seemed deserted and you could feel the kiss of doom as soon as you entered the vast foyer. That foyer was really something, mostly marble and with a grand staircase leading up to the auditorium. In fact, the foyer with its bars and refreshment rooms, was larger than the auditorium!" *Mr P.W.*

Electric Theatre
(later Savoy), Rendezvous Street

This was Folkestone's first place of entertainment wholly devoted to moving pictures. The building was originally started as a music hall, but became a garage then a roller skating rink. The conversion to a cinema was by architect R.A. Bowles and local builder Otto Marx. The main external feature, beneath some highly decorative plasterwork, was an ornamental glass canopy extending over the adjacent pavement bearing the words ELECTRIC THEATRE picked out in stained glass on the front, and OPEN 3 TO 10.30 on either side. Passersby were informed additionally of the theatre's location by a sign suspended over the canopy facing up and down the street.

THE FOLKESTONE EXPRESS was most enthusiastic about the new venture: 'It has a most attractive front to the main thoroughfare and in every way it is smart. After passing through the outer doors there is a nice entresol and half a dozen heavily-carpeted stairs lead to the theatre which is elegantly decorated and fitted and gives a pleasant feeling of comfort and luxury'.

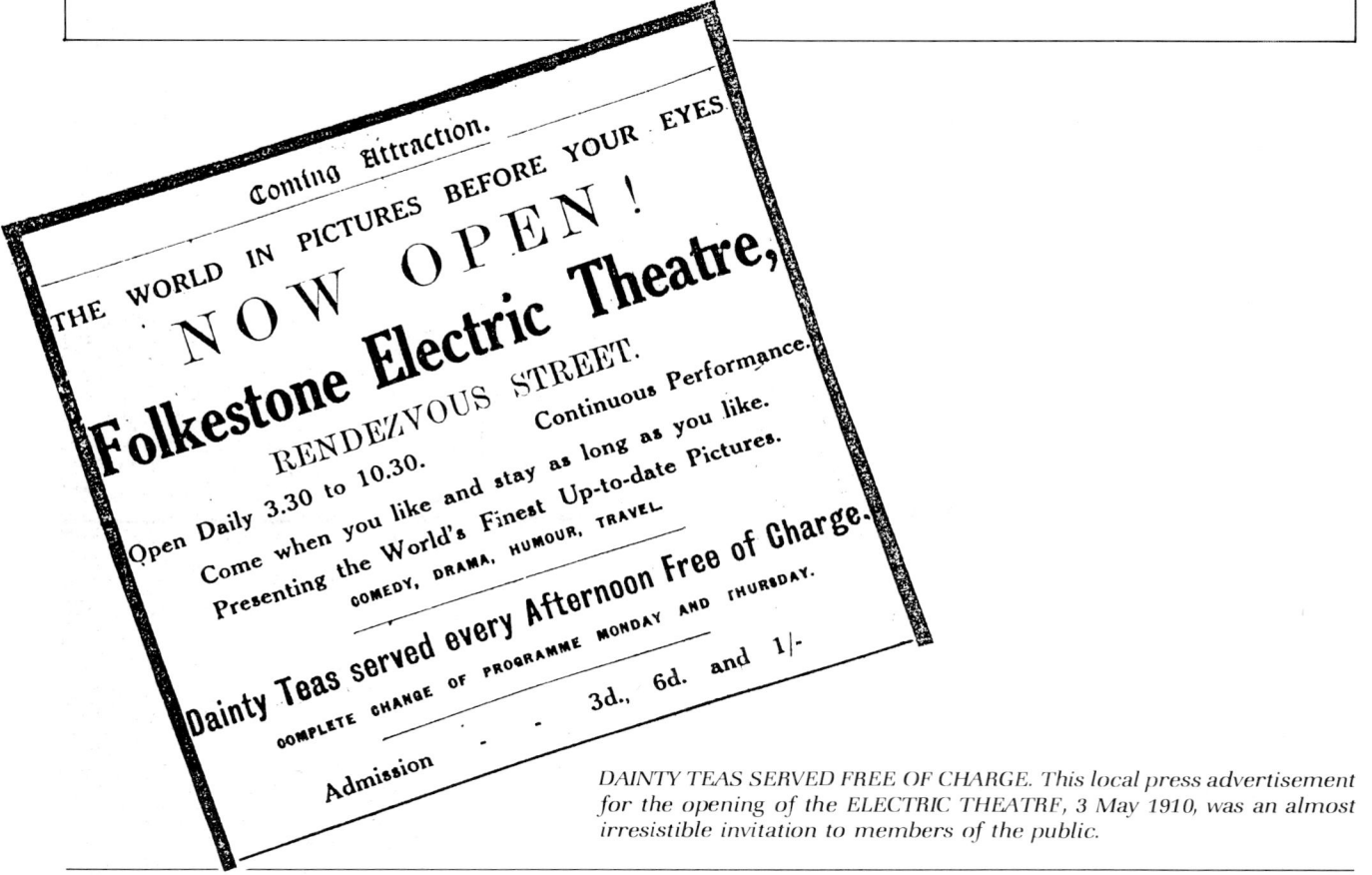

DAINTY TEAS SERVED FREE OF CHARGE. This local press advertisement for the opening of the ELECTRIC THEATRE, 3 May 1910, was an almost irresistible invitation to members of the public.

The Grand Opening of the ELECTRIC THEATRE was on Tuesday, 3 May 1910, with a special performance of a number of interesting films, including coloured pictures by Pathé Freres. The manager, J.C. Caffrey, welcomed members of the Folkestone Corporation and other townspeople. Seating for 400 was on one level, prices being 3d, 6d and 1/-d. Patrons entered the cinema from the street at the screen end, the projection box being at the rear of the hall. Performances were continuous: 'COME WHEN YOU LIKE, STAY AS LONG AS YOU LIKE', proclaimed the management. 'The world's finest picture plays' would be shown and there would be a complete change of programmes on Mondays and Thursdays. An added inducement at matinee performances was that 'Dainty Teas' would be served free of charge.

The ELECTRIC THEATRE proved very popular. By 1928 it had been re-named the SAVOY and in that year scooped the opposition by announcing: 'NEXT WEEK, THE TALKING FILMS - FIRST CINEMA TO BE INSTALLED IN KENT'. Commented a local paper: 'A start has been made in filming a person singing and dancing, but it is expected that soon an ordinary film will be made which, when screened, will produce the artistes' conversation continuously throughout the film....' Indeed, such things would come to pass.

FOLKESTONE ELECTRIC THEATRE
RENDEZVOUS STREET.

LIEUT. DARING AND THE MIDDLE-WEIGHT CHAMPION.
Another of the popular hero's exciting adventures.

THE OASIS OF GABES,
Splendid coloured views of the oasis; hundreds of camels preparing to cross the desert; views near Tripoli.

THE SPIDER'S WEB.
A very powerful Vitagraph drama.

A GOOD TONIC,
One of the best comic pictures shown for a long time.

Tea served every afternoon from 4 to 5 free of charge.

THE JAMES BOND OF 1912. Lieut. Daring was the hero of a series of exciting adventure films made by the pioneering Walthamstow studios of British and Colonial Films. The advertisement of 24 August 1912 (above) features LIEUT. DARING AND THE MIDDLEWEIGHT CHAMPION at the ELECTRIC THEATRE, the poster alongside being for LIEUT. DARING AND THE PHOTOGRAPHING PIGEON! As for THE SPIDER'S WEB, also in the programme of films, this is described as a powerful Vitagraph drama. 'Vitagraph' was one of the early Hollywood studios and its stars included Norma Talmadge and comedian Larry Semon, both of whom became famous.

The ELECTRIC THEATRE in 1912. The ornamental glass canopy was a feature particularly favoured by architect A.R. BOWLES and it appears in other halls of the period in Canterbury, Hythe and Folkestone.

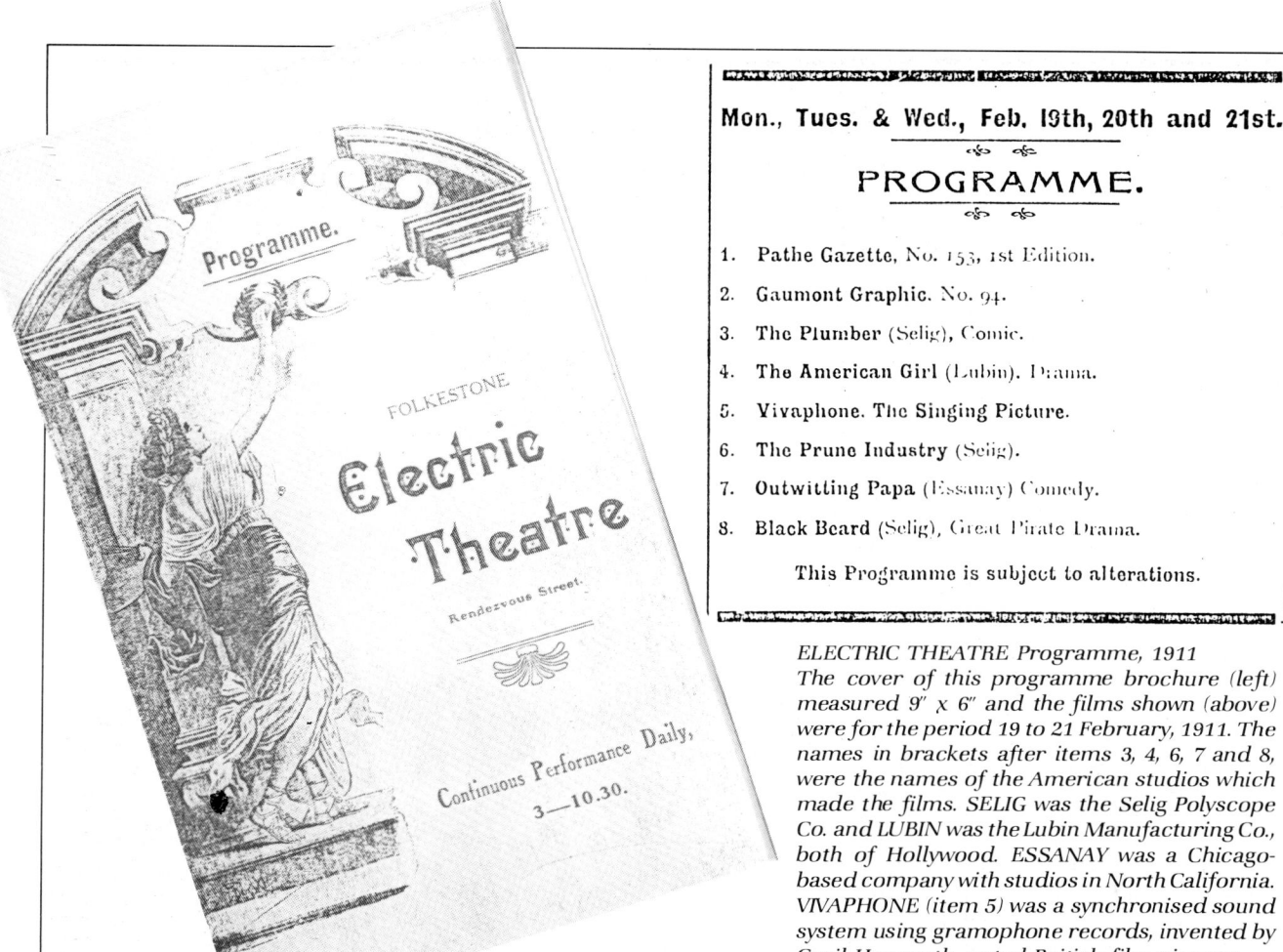

Mon., Tues. & Wed., Feb. 19th, 20th and 21st.

PROGRAMME.

1. Pathe Gazette, No. 153, 1st Edition.
2. Gaumont Graphic. No. 94.
3. The Plumber (Selig), Comic.
4. The American Girl (Lubin). Drama.
5. Vivaphone. The Singing Picture.
6. The Prune Industry (Selig).
7. Outwitting Papa (Essanay) Comedy.
8. Black Beard (Selig), Great Pirate Drama.

This Programme is subject to alterations.

ELECTRIC THEATRE Programme, 1911
The cover of this programme brochure (left) measured 9" x 6" and the films shown (above) were for the period 19 to 21 February, 1911. The names in brackets after items 3, 4, 6, 7 and 8, were the names of the American studios which made the films. SELIG was the Selig Polyscope Co. and LUBIN was the Lubin Manufacturing Co., both of Hollywood. ESSANAY was a Chicago-based company with studios in North California. VIVAPHONE (item 5) was a synchronised sound system using gramophone records, invented by Cecil Hepworth, noted British film pioneer.

In October 1928, the SAVOY screened *FIRE*. It was complete with full effects, lighting and sound, with a specially augmented orchestra. What it proved to be was virtually a trailer for the 'Great Savoy Inferno', a real-life drama which shocked Folkestone. The headlines in the local newspaper graphically tell of that fateful day, 13 December 1928: 'Savoy Theatre gutted.... Tongues of Flame Shoot 40ft in Air.... Damage Estimated at £6,000.... Talking Apparatus Saved.' It seems that the fire had taken hold of the building at the stage-end, and although the rear wall stood, it was split from top to bottom by the heat.

The decision to re-build the cinema was taken even before the smoke had cleared and early in 1929 work was started on the NEW SAVOY SUPER CINEMA which opened in June of the same year (see section on the NEW SAVOY).

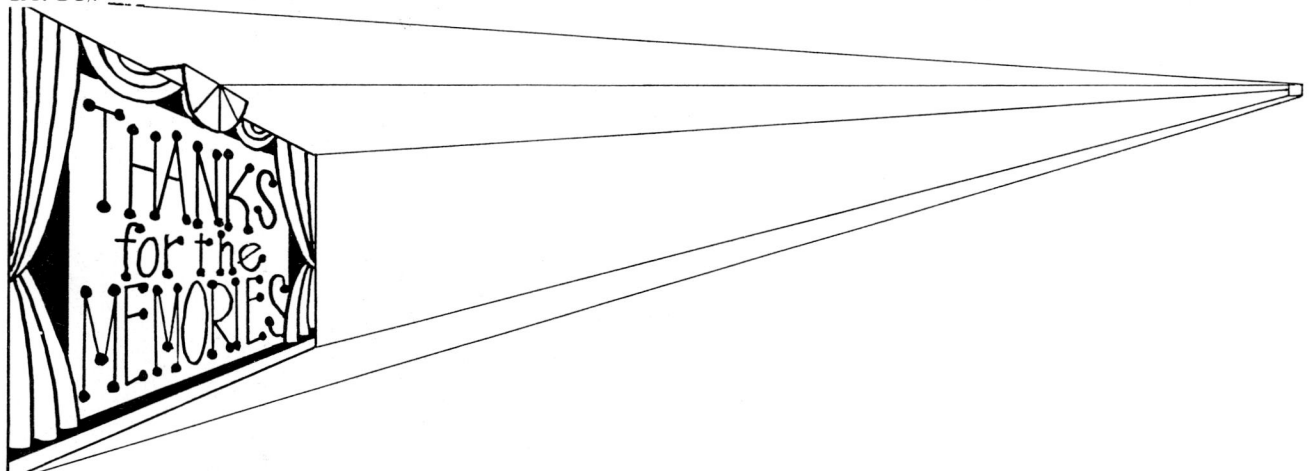

"I was a six-year old at the time of the SAVOY fire. I was getting excited about Christmas and I was out window-shopping at Plummers with my mother. It seemed a really big fire and I remember it gutted the cinema. The only other thing I remember about the SAVOY was the installation of an expanding screen, one that expanded vertically but not, I think, horizontally. But one thing I did object to was the SAVOY practice of spraying their patrons with a pungent, perfumed disinfectant, presumably in the interests of hygiene." *Mr P.W.*

Cheriton Electric Hall
(later Palace Theatre), Cheriton High Street

'If you have not seen the pictures presented at the above hall, then you have not seen the best' claimed manager W.F. Marlow when the ELECTRIC HALL opened on 11 August, 1911. A.O. Sherren was the designer of this purpose-built cinema, the contractors being Hayward and Paramor Ltd.

The local press considered it an attractive building externally, with rough-cast front and handsome pillars to the main entrance, surmounted by a large dome. The interior was luxuriously furnished and the 400 seats were mainly of the plush tip-up kind. Whilst appearance and comfort were prime considerations, the management made a point of emphasising that the building was practically fireproof and conformed to the Cinematograph Act of 1909.

Mr Reginald W. Tedhams went to the ELECTRIC HALL as a teenager in 1914, his job being to sell programmes and sweets. But before long he had been promoted to assistant projectionist and he recalls projecting *THE ADVENTURES OF PEARL WHITE*, his favourite silent serial. On one occasion the film caught fire, but Mr Tedhams quickly threw a wet blanket over the projector and extinguished the flames. Prices of admission were 6d, 9d and 1/-d, reduced to only 2d on Saturday afternoons.

During the first world war, the ELECTRIC HALL was well patronised by soldiers from Shorncliffe Camp, live entertainment being added to the twice-nightly bill, including vaudeville, boxing and wrestling. In the twenties there was a change of name to THE PALACE THEATRE, large hoardings being erected to the left of the entrance, showing posters and a huge inscription: VAUDEVILLE & PICTURES TONIGHT. It was clear that a struggle for survival was in process, but the battle was lost with the theatre closing down in 1923.

In 1924 it became a warehouse.

HEAVY ADVERTISING accompanied the change of name to THE PALACE THEATRE.

Open-Air Cinema
Linden Crescent

This was described as THE FIRST DAY AND NIGHT CINEMA IN EUROPE and was operated by the Open Air Cinema Company who were backed by Keith Prowse. The first performance was on 29 May 1912, the venue being a tented structure. 'The show will accommodate 500 people who can sit in the open air on a beautiful summer's day with the sky as a covering and watch the romance, tragedy and comedy enacted on the screen in perfect comfort' declared the management, adding 'In wet weather, a sliding canvas roof can be drawn along the top.'

The following month, the local press tried to boost the enterprise but only succeeded in drawing attention to the more unattractive aspects of open-air filmgoing:-

> 'Despite the chill and rain, many find real comfort in sitting beneath the huge canvas top on pleasant evenings, as well as on rainy ones, as they watch the picture. Few people are aware that the audience can keep perfectly dry underneath the canvas top'.

By the autumn of 1912, THE OPEN AIR CINEMA had disappeared from the Folkestone scene, beaten by the English climate.

Open-Air Cinema.   Linden Crescent.

The FIRST Day and Night CINEMA in Europe!

Prices: 3d, 6d. & 1/-

Did You Guess It?

IT SUGGESTS HEALTH.   IT KEEPS YOU COOL.

Opens Wednesday, May 29th.   2.30 to 10.30 p.m.   Handsome Souvenirs.
(No. 3)

'TEASER' ADVERTISING was used to arouse interest in the OPEN AIR CINEMA before it opened. The final advertisement in the series appeared in the FOLKESTONE HERALD of 25 May, 1912 (above).

Queen's Cinema
Tontine Street

Folkestone filmgoers first learnt of a proposed picture house in Tontine Street in June 1911 when an anonymous correspondent in a local newspaper wrote:

'One is reluctant to interfere with local enterprise, but the interests of the public have a claim for consideration. The projected new picture palace in Tontine Street has had the pavement closed for several weeks past, but so far as can been seen, all that has been done to its exterior is the picking out of the mortar between the bricks, work that should not have necessitated the closing of the pavement for a quarter of the time taken. The sooner this is remedied the sooner the convenience of the public can be adjusted.'

Not until March 1912 did the Watch Committee approve 79 Tontine Street for cinematograph purposes. The property, previously occupied by Richard Court, coal and coke merchant, was converted into an Electric Picture Palace, opening in June of that year as the QUEEN'S CINEMA.

The 400-seater theatre was promoted as an 'excellently equipped hall.... the floor slopes upwards to the back.... tip-top plush seats are provided for all.' Manager Hugh Bevan made a great point that up-to-date cinematograph machines had been installed which were 'not worked by hand but by motor'. And that pianist Fred Leppard who accompanied the silent pictures of the day, played extremely well!

Unfortunately there were complaints from some patrons about their view of the screen and later the local press reported that 'the pillars which at present obstruct the view of a few people are to be removed and large iron girders placed across the hall'. In October 1912 seat prices at 6d, 4d and 2d were being advertised.

By 1914 the property had passed to Robert Forsyth who, with his brother Lloyd, had been organising entertainment on the Victoria Pier for some years, although the hall there proved too small to be profitable. The QUEEN'S was open throughout the years of the first world war but appears to have closed towards the end of 1917, when the single-storey building was adapted for other uses.

DO COME MORE OFTEN! That was the object of this THREE CHANGES WEEKLY advert in the local press of 15 June, 1912.

QUEEN'S CINEMA,
TONTINE STREET, FOLKESTONE.

WORLD'S LATEST PICTURES.

THREE CHANGES WEEKLY.

Daily at 4 and 8.

Special Childrens Matinee Saturday at 2.30.

Plush tip-up seats all parts.

Latest Pictures from Pathe's Gazette.

POPULAR PRICES.

HUGH BEVAN, Manager.

CONVERTED TO DWELLING ACCOMMODATION. The QUEEN'S CINEMA building in 1987.

The Playhouse
Guildhall Street

> T H E P L A Y H O U S E,
> GUILDHALL STREET.
>
> Continual Cinematograph Entertainment,
> Daily 2.30 to 10.30.
> SEE NEW PLAY.
> Delightful Music.
> The most Luxurious TEA ROOMS on the South Coast.
> Change of Programme Monday and Thursday.
> Admission 3d., 6d., 1s., 1s. 6d.
>
> PLAYHOUSE TEA ROOM,
> (Open to the Public apart from the Theatre).
> Handsomely appointed.
> Lunches, Teas, Evening Cafe, Lounge.
> Open 11 a.m. to 10 p.m.

CONFUSING. This press advert of 24 August, 1912, bears the invitation SEE NEW PLAY. But it was a film.

The success of the ELECTRIC THEATRE encouraged the proprietors to build a second cinema in Folkestone. Ivy House, a double-fronted residence and livery stables was purchased and then demolished. This provided an excellent site for the 'most perfectly equipped Cinematograph Theatre in the Kingdom' which was to be built there.

A.R. Bowles was again the architect chosen to design the new cinema, which proved to be a very substantial building faced with Bath stone, its attractive appearance being enhanced by a five-pointed star above the large letters below, which read THE PLAYHOUSE. The cinema's name was repeated in stained glass letters along the top of the glass canopy (described in the local press as a 'pretty ironwork porch, illuminated by electricity and adorned with flowers') supported by four slender cast-iron pillars which extended over a marble-floored area.

Patrons entered the cinema through one of the two pairs of ornate doors leading to the foyer and auditorium. 'The vestibule is handsome and imposing' commented a local newspaper, 'and a wide stairway leads to a fine balcony. Thick pile carpet covers the whole of the floor and there is not a sound from patrons passing in and out'. Readers were further informed that electricity was installed and that the lighting brackets contained three globes, the outer ones being white lights and the inner ones being red, the latter for use when the pictures were being shown. The writer concluded by saying that 'the decoration of the ceiling and the transparency work through which the light shines are very effective; the pictures are of old masters'.

INTERIOR OF THE PLAYHOUSE, c.1937. Behind the curtains a 17ft-deep stage was provided where, in the days of the silent films, variety acts entertained audiences between pictures. Of special interest is the low ceiling and the ornamental plasterwork.

EXTERIOR OF THE PLAYHOUSE, c.1937. The exterior of the theatre changed little over the years whilst the name, PLAYHOUSE, remained until the end. The ornamental glass canopy identifies the architect, A.R. BOWLES, who designed the ELECTRIC THEATRE (later SAVOY), Folkestone.

THE PLAYHOUSE seated 732 people (permission for a 1000-seater theatre originally envisaged by the architect had been vetoed by the Town Council), admission prices ranging from 3d in the front stalls to 1/6d in the best seats in the balcony. A special attraction for patrons was a luxurious tea-room on the first floor which seated 50 and was furnished throughout in splendid style by Bobbys, the local department store. Light refreshments at popular prices could be obtained from 11 in the morning until 11 at night, a service which was greatly appreciated and well patronised.

The new cinema opened on the afternoon of Wednesday 14 August 1912, and was something of an occasion. The programme of silent pictures included an early version of TREASURE ISLAND and a packed house put its seal of approval on THE PLAYHOUSE. Before long the cinema had its own attractive programme headed: PLAYHOUSE SUPER CINEMA & CAFE, FOLKESTONE, with a picture of its distinctive frontage on the cover.

In 1929 entrepreneur Walter Bentley took over THE PLAYHOUSE and immediately arranged for the installation of a Compton organ, the first in Folkestone. It was a 2 manual/5 rank model, with a fixed console, the opening organist, J.I.Taylor, playing to an enthusiastic audience. Another 'first' that year, was the screening of a full-length sound film called LUCKY BOY with George Jessel. However, the sound apparatus had been rented for the occasion and not until December 1929 were talking pictures featured regularly at THE PLAYHOUSE, initially with silent films in support.

When war came in September 1939, THE PLAYHOUSE remained open, but at the height of the Battle of Britain in July 1940 it closed down and did not re-open until April 1946. The following year a season of foreign language films drew the crowds, but thereafter attendances declined until in 1962 the cinema closed for good. It was demolished in 1963 to make way for a supermarket, currently empty. Sadly, the Compton organ was demolished with the building.

PLAYHOUSE PROGRAMME (reduced size) This was the August 1929 cover. Later a combined PLAYHOUSE and CENTRAL Monthly Review was published.

A MONTH BEFORE CLOSURE this advertisement appeared in the FOLKESTONE HERALD, 1 June 1940. The double-bill programme lasted 3¼ hours and included the popular Pathé Gazette.

84

The Central Picture Theatre
George Lane
(later known as the Essoldo, Curzon and Classic and, currently, Cannon)

The old and the new came together when, in 1912, THE CENTRAL PICTURE THEATRE was built on an historic site which formed part of the ancient ballium from which the adjacent Bayle takes its name. The architect was H. Vivian who, to form the canopied entrance to the theatre, found it necessary to remove the shops in George Lane whilst, at the same time, retaining the dwelling apartments on the first and other floors.

A centrally-sited exterior paybox was located immediately below the ornamental canopy which bore the words THE CENTRAL PICTURE THEATRE picked out in stained glass lettering and, having bought their tickets, patrons could proceed to a tea and refreshment bar with ceiling decorations in the Adam style and admire the warm red colour scheme. Proceeding to the 85ft long auditorium which was lit by eight cluster lamps in the ceiling, filmgoers found themselves in a world dominated by shades of light and dark blue.

The theatre was described as "The most luxurious in the town or district, perfectly ventilated and with splendid sanitation" and seated 750 people. For 1/-d patrons could enjoy the armchair comfort of the fauteuils, whilst 6d purchased a seat in the stalls. The front seats cost only 3d and were doubtless wooden.

The opening attraction for week commencing 23 September, 1912, was a 'colossal cinedrama' entitled *THE MYSTERIES OF PARIS*, live music being presented by the resident Arcadians orchestra. The following week, *NELLIE THE LION TAMER* was the main attraction, supported by 'an exceptionally fine Indian Picture' called *BEFORE THE WHITE MAN CAME*. In October, there was *THE LION TAMER'S REVENGE*, but whether Nellie was still the lion tamer concerned is not at all clear.

Over the years THE CENTRAL prospered and in 1921 it was decided to increase the seating capacity by literally raising the roof. The jacking-up process was accomplished by a mass of interior scaffolding (see photograph) enabling the required brick courses to be added, first one side then the other. Finally, a new balcony was constructed and the projection room was moved up one floor, resulting in the theatre's capacity being increased to around 1500. It should be mentioned that having climbed the steeply-raked slope to the faraway second balcony, patrons soon discovered that the screen appeared very distant as if viewed through the wrong end of a telescope.

Western Electric sound equipment was installed in October, 1929, the first sound feature film being *BULLDOG DRUMMOND* with Ronald Colman in the title role. There followed the boom years of the thirties and business was even better during the war years, 1939-1945. THE CENTRAL was one of the two theatres in Folkestone which remained open throughout the conflict and although few civilians could be seen in the audience due to evacuation, the Armed Forces of the Crown more than made up for the absent residents.

The post-war years saw diminishing audiences and in November 1973 the theatre was closed so that it could be converted to a triple-screen complex. Work proceeded slowly and it was not until March 1974 that the first two screens were opened to the public, the third screen becoming available in May 1974.

For most of its long life, the theatre in George Lane has been known as THE CENTRAL, but over the years changes in ownership have resulted in changes of name: ESSOLDO, CURZON, CLASSIC and currently CANNON, still with 3 screens. The seating capacities for Screens 1, 2 and 3 are respectively 291, 308 and 196, to make a total of 795 seats. The CANNON is the sole surviving cinema operating in Folkestone.

THE CENTRAL PICTURE THEATRE.
EXTERIOR prior to 1921, when the theatre was modernised. The paybox is centrally sited outside the building in the American tradition. The dwelling accommodation, originally over shop premises, is still in position. The unknown figure is doubtless the manager - and very smart he looks too.
INTERIOR, also prior to 1921. Note the low ceiling, the curtained windows on the left and the orchestra pit.

RAISING THE ROOF OF THE CENTRAL PICTURE THEATRE, 1921. This remarkable photograph shows the erection of scaffolding in the interior of the cinema (see text). It was stated to be the highest interior scaffolding ever erected in Folkestone and reached a height of 70ft.

THE INTERIOR OF THE CENTRAL, c.1937. The upper photograph is looking towards the proscenium. The side seats have been retained, but the orchestra pit, being no longer required, has been removed.

The lower photograph gives a view to the rear of the cinema and shows the first and second balconies. Note the high roof.

CONGRESS DANCES was shown at the CENTRAL in 1931 and starred Conrad Veidt and Lilian Harvey. The display (above) appeared in Bobby's front window, the artist being Dudley Pout (see 'Thanks for the Memories', GRANADA, Dover). The supplementary notice read: 'Music from the film now being played by Bobby's Orchestra in the Café.'

WORLD PREMIERE OF 'KIPPS'
This took place at the CENTRAL on the evening of 12 May 1941, with the Mayor introducing the stars of the film: Diana Wynyard, Phyllis Calvert and Michael Redgrave. Later, in their honour, there was a Film Star Ball at the Leas Cliff Hall, followed by supper at the Queens Hotel. All of this was filmed by the MOVIETONE NEWS cameramen as part of the publicity drive to promote the film in the U.S.A.

EXTERIOR OF THE CENTRAL PICTURE THEATRE, c.1937, then part of the Union Cinemas circuit. The paybox has been moved to inside the theatre, the hanging gas lamps have vanished and the Manager of the day is nowhere to be seen, as in the previous photograph.

Thanks for the Memories

Behind the Beam at the Central

"I was evacuated from Folkestone to Wales in 1940 and one night was shown round the projection room of the Gaiety Cinema, Cardiff. I was captivated by this world of machinery, valves and meters, not to mention the all-pervading smell of peardrops from the film cement used to join up broken film. Later during my sojourn I managed to worm my way into the projection room of the Electric Cinema, Merthyr Tydfil, where I was taught to lace-up projectors, re-wind films and generally make myself useful.

This experience was to hold me in good stead when I returned to Folkestone and left school at the age of 15. I felt I must work in the cinema industry and nervously asked to see the manager of the CENTRAL, a Mr Foulds. After some piercing questions he started me as third projectionist at 35 shillings a week (£1.75). This was quite good considering that a trademan's wages in Folkestone at the time was around £4 a week.

I soon discovered that there were no set hours of work. We started at 10am and finished at 10.30pm or when the show ended. Meal breaks were taken in shifts, although if it was a late start (after 1pm) we all went to lunch at the same time, about 11.30am. Tea breaks started at 4pm and lasted one hour, when most of us went home for a meal. By tradition the person-in-charge took the last tea break at 6pm. Supper-time was half an hour, the older members going to the pub for a pint. The chief projectionist usually had the last supper break which meant he only re-appeared at the end of the show. This was a tradition I was glad to maintain when I became chief projectionist some ten years later.

The film was delivered in 1000ft reels which we doubled-up on one spool to give about 20 minutes running time on one projector. We then changed over to the next projector for 20 minutes and so on through the day. The average film was about 10 reels though epics might take 14 or more reels. The chief projectionist would show reels 1-2, the next in line 3-4 and so on. There were usually three of us on duty during the day, so you would run one, lace, and carbon up the arc of the projector after the reel was finished. You could then have a 'reel rest', although when meal breaks started, it was every other reel. If you were careful about exactly when you went to tea and when you came back, you could manipulate which reels you ran. The aim was to fiddle yourself a single reel which counted as your reel.

We worked 5 days a week, or should I say 5½ days. We were allowed one full day off and half a day from 1pm. There was no such thing then as extra pay for Sundays and Bank Holidays, so if your day off fell on those days you considered yourself lucky. Cinemas in Folkestone were allowed to open from 2pm on a Sunday, which counted as a normal working day; in fact, Sunday was very hard work because we ran old films which were in a disgraceful condition. These prints had to be carefully checked because if they broke in the projector there was an immediate risk of fire. Celluloid burns fiercely and it is a wonder that there were not more fires in cinema projection rooms generally. The last nitrate film was issued in May 1952, after which the risks were greatly reduced.

I have served in many cinemas since those wartime years but will always remember my time at the CENTRAL with great affection and gratitude."

Len Petts

Mr Len Petts at a BTH projector, Folkestone ODEON, 1951

Thanks for the Memories

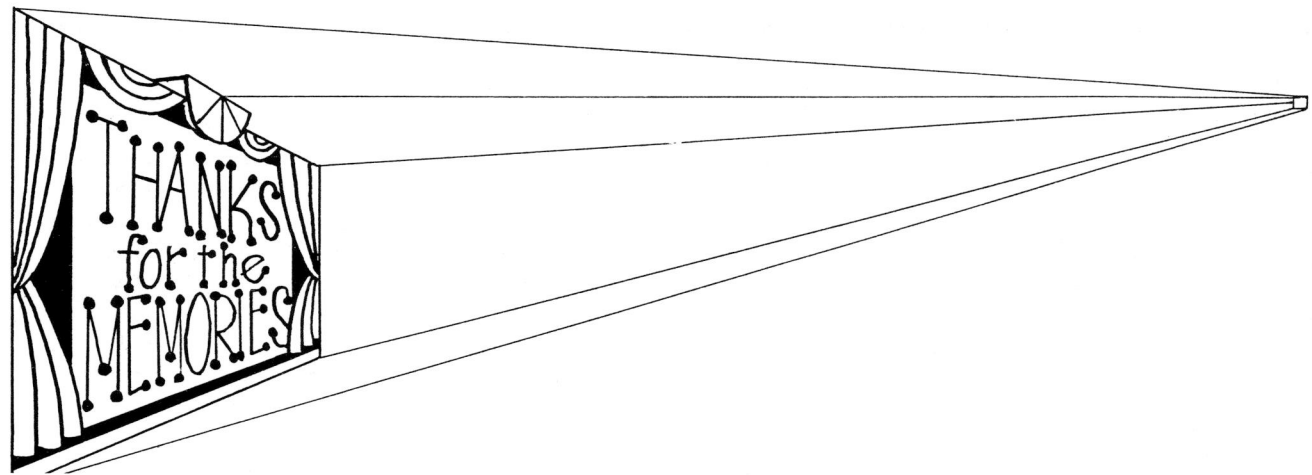

"My earliest recollection of the CENTRAL cinema in George Lane stems from pre-war days when we kids used to haunt the place. The entrance in those days consisted of two main pairs of doors resplendant with bevelled glass panels and shining brass kick-plates, not forgetting the glossy (mahogany, I think) doors themselves. The 'lesser' patrons who could only brandish the odd 4d or 6d admission, had to enter by a lower passage just to the left of the frontage where there was a rather high (or was it because I was only little in those days?) window, similar to the small type of window at most railway station booking offices. The girl cashier sat on a swivel seat and would swing round to issue a ticket, but only after serving the needs of more affluent patrons on the 'posh' side. In those halcyon days of the cinema, the front stalls extended as close as possible to the screen in order to 'pack 'em in'. The screen at the CENTRAL was pretty high and I often went home with a stiff neck.

Whereas the flooring of the SAVOY and ASTORIA/ODEON balconies were constructed in steps, at the CENTRAL the floor sloped. This could be dangerous, especially in the upper balcony if you were wearing a new pair of shoes. Marjorie Jordan, a former 'Ice Cream' girl who was employed there, told me of the time she was walking backwards down the aisle when she tripped over someone's feet which were sticking out into the aisle, with the result that she fell over backwards, ice creams flying in all directions, plus her 17/6d 'float'. You couldn't really say that she had found her Eldorado!

My wife's aunt used to relate how in the days of the silent films at the CENTRAL, she stood, as a young girl, by the pianist telling him what mood of music he should play, for he was in fact blind. He was always referred to as 'Blind Marsh'."

Mr E.R.H.

"To the best of my recollection it was at the CENTRAL that I saw *HENRY V* with that great actor Laurence Olivier.

The battle scenes were truly awesome and I can still hear the swish of the arrows from the English bows as they soared into the air before descending upon the French soldiers, turning the tide of battle.

Although I had seen Olivier in *WUTHERING HEIGHTS* and *REBECCA* in the early years of the war, they do not compare with *HENRY V*, in my opinion. I had to wait until 1955 before Olivier reached the heights again, and that was in *RICHARD III*, which also starred John Gielgud and Ralph Richardson, firm favourites of mine.

Oddly enough, I cannot stand Shakespeare on the stage...."

Mr C.E.

Laurence Olivier in HENRY V.

The Twenties

Talking pictures arrived in 1928 and when *THE JAZZ SINGER* was shown in London in September of that year, a new era had dawned for the film industry. The only new cinema opened in Folkestone during this period was the SAVOY, built on the site of the old cinema which had been destroyed by fire.

The new Savoy Cinema

'Risen from the ashes of the old building which was destroyed by fire last December, the new Savoy Theatre opened in a blaze of splendour on Saturday' ran the opening paragraph in the FOLKESTONE HERALD in July 1929 following the gala opening on 29 June attended by the Mayor and local dignatories. The silent film drama they watched starred Sir John Martin Harvey and was entitled *THE BURGOMASTER OF STILEMONDE*. John Russell and his orchestra provided the musical accompaniment as well as Percy Milton at the newly-installed Dutch-built Standaart organ.

The exterior of the new SAVOY proved something of a disappointment to many of the previous patrons, who missed the splendid glass canopy which had been a distinctive feature of the old building. They also found that the stage and screen were now sited at the far end of the auditorium and there was a balcony, raising the total seating capacity to 932, double that of the old cinema. On the first floor there was a café and palm lounge, incorporating a soda fountain and ice-cream buffet. The walls of the auditorium were of a delicately-tinted marblecote, whilst the ceiling was painted to resemble a sky of azure-blue flecked with clouds. The management proclaimed that 'perfect ventilation, view, projection, seating and harmony equals 100% entertainment' and patrons agreed that it was indeed a vast improvement on the previous cinema.

Whilst silent films were screened in July and August 1929, in September *BROADWAY MELODY* became the first feature-length sound film to be screened at the SAVOY. Then came *SHOWBOAT*, *THE SINGING FOOL*, *CHASING RAINBOWS*, starring Charles King who made a personal appearance at the SAVOY, *ALL QUIET ON THE WESTERN FRONT* and *RIO RITA*, all of which played to packed houses.

In 1933, Dover Entertainments Ltd. (Lessees of the KING'S HALL, Dover) took over and decided to feature the Standaart organ which had seen so little service since the Talkies arrived. In May 1934 the organ was moved from the side of the orchestra pit to a central position and Reginald Foort, the famous broadcasting organist, inaugurated a season of live music. George Pattman and Frank Newman also made guest appearances at the theatre.

When war came, the SAVOY remained open until 27 July 1940, when it closed after the last performance on that day. However, on 13 May, 1941, the Mayor and Mayoress of Folkestone attended the GRAND RE-OPENING of the cinema, when *THE GHOST TRAIN*, starring Arthur Askey, was shown to a packed house in which uniforms predominated. Business continued to be good during the war years, since for members of HMF in particular, cinemas were a haven of comfort and escapism.

With peace came the gradual disappearance of patrons in uniform and the spread of TV accelerated the decline in attendances. In October 1961 Bingo sessions were introduced and when the cinema became the Star Social Club, films were shown no more. Today the oldest theatre in Folkestone stands empty.

SAVOY

Phone 4666.   Daily From 2 p.m.

GRAND RE-OPENING

TUESDAY, MAY 13
at 6 p.m.
All Seats Bookable In Advance.

On the Screen.

ARTHUR   RICHARD
(BIG HEARTED)   (STINKER)
ASKEY   MURDOCH

THE
GHOST TRAIN
At 2.0, 4.50, 8.30.   (a)

RICHARD   ANDY
ARLEN   DEVINE

HOT STEEL
At 3.30, 6.20.   (a)

On the House.
FUN and GAMES
Commere   Compere   Commere
Betty Carter   Fred Allwood   Gerda Kaye

Edward O'Henry at the Organ.

SUNDAY, MAY 18th —
The Crazy Gang in
ALF'S BUTTON AFLOAT
Joan Bennett and Doug. Fairbanks in
GREEN HELL

THIS GRAND RE-OPENING PROGRAMME was presented on 13th May, 1941, the SAVOY having been closed in July 1940 at the height of the Blitz. Besides the two films there was a stage presentation (of sorts) and Edward O'Henry at the Standaart organ.

EXTERIOR OF THE NEW SAVOY CINEMA, c.1955. The unimaginative facade compares unfavourably with that of the original ELECTRIC THEATRE.

PERCY MILTON at the console of the Standaart organ, 1930.

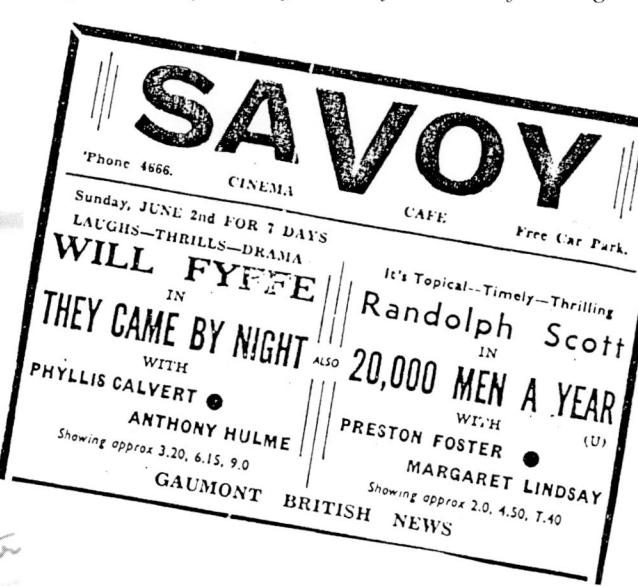

TYPICAL DOUBLE BILL at the SAVOY, week commencing 2nd June, 1940, one month before the cinema closed because of the Blitz. The names of the leading players in the two films will be known to many readers of this book.

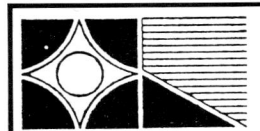

The Thirties

Astoria
(later Odeon), Sandgate Road

As Folkestone is a seaside resort specialising in entertainment for its visitors, it is perhaps surprising that Dover's super-cinema, the GRANADA, opened four years ahead of the ASTORIA. However, of the three towns covered in this book, Deal was the last in the super-cinema field, the ODEON being opened on 25 July, 1936.

It was in January 1934 that the citizens of Folkestone learnt that they were losing Maestrani's Central Resaurant, long established in the town, and that in its place would rise a new super cinema complete with licensed restaurant and bar. Folkestone was proud of the fact that the ASTORIA super cinema would be a local enterprise and not just one more cinema to be built by the circuit giants.

MAESTRANI'S RESTAURANT AT 24 & 26 SANDGATE ROAD, demolished to provide the site of the ASTORIA. Mr G.F. Ronco, the proprietor became a member of the board of ASTORIA (FOLKESTONE) LTD.

The architect/designer for the ASTORIA was Edward A. Stone, well-known for his four London Astoria cinema designs, particularly the Finsbury Park Astoria, who joined the board of Astoria (Folkestone) Ltd, a locally-controlled private company. Managing Director of the company and the main driving force was Major C.H. Bell, who was also the consulting engineer. The main contractor was Mr O. Marx. The cost of the building was £55,000 exclusive of site; the overall figure was put at £100,000.

ASTORIA

SEATING ACCOMMODATION - Stalls 1,120; Front Balcony 160; Back Balcony 390; Total 1,670.

EXTERIOR - Walls, patent concrete surface finish, hammered and tooled below balcony level. Windows, metal, painted green. Canopy, concrete and sherardised metal with panelled effects and giving space for lights. Entrance doors, laminated hardwood, with flush black surface.

AUDITORIUM - Walls, stone texture paint. Columns, pink, gold and grey. Proscenium curtain: white as a background for artificial lighting effects. Orchestra grilles and handrails, metal, of oval section, painted cream. Organ grille, vertical lines of plaster, with spaces between.

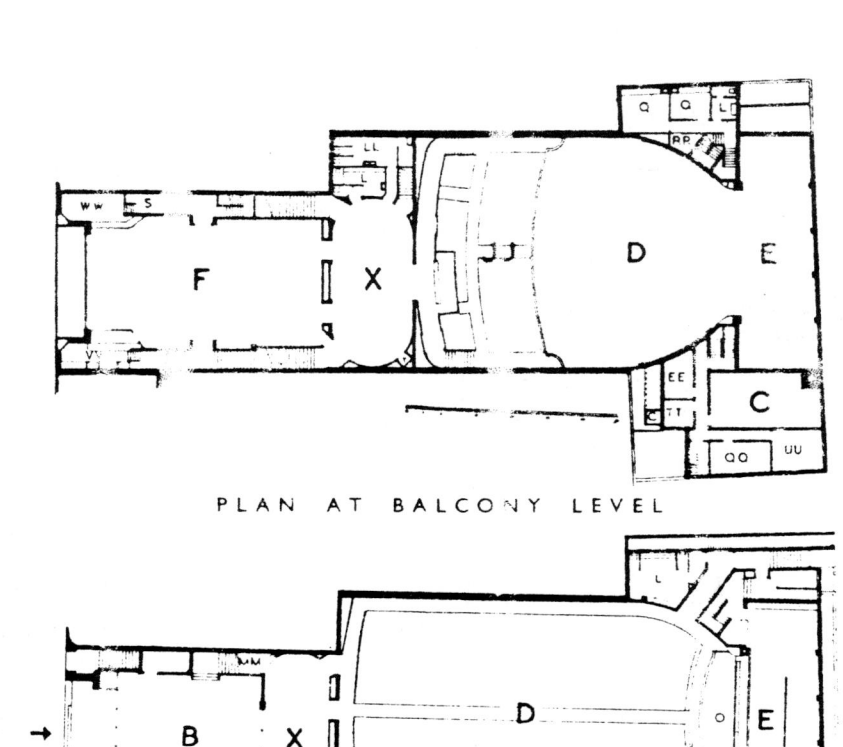

PLAN AT BALCONY LEVEL

PLAN OF ENTRANCE HALL AND STALLS

LONGITUDINAL SECTION

B, Entrance Hall.
BB, Staff Room.
C, Ventilation.
D, Auditorium.
E, Stage.
EE, Organ Chamber.
F, Café.
G, Projection Room.
JJ, Balcony.
K, Waiting Space.
L, Men's Lavatory.
LL, Women's Lavatory.
M, Management.
MM, Cloaks.
O, Orchestra.
Q, Dressing Room.
QQ, Rewinding Room.
RR, Horn Chamber.
S, Store.
TT, Organ Blower.
UU, Battery Room.
V, Pay Office.
WW, Snack Bar.
X, Foyer.

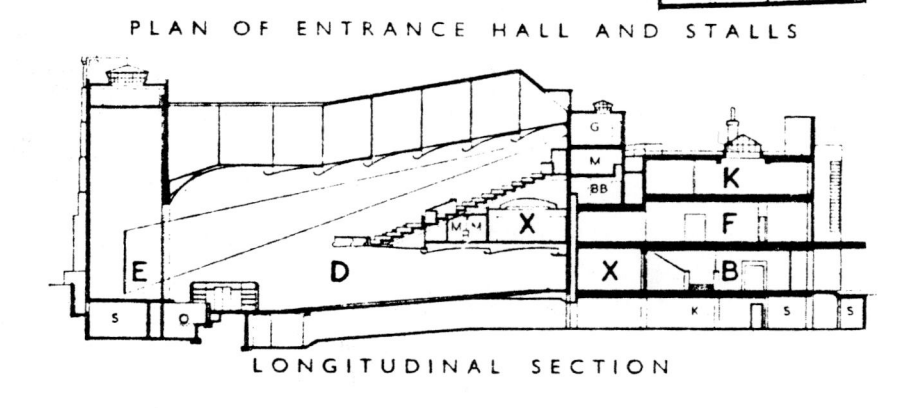

PLANS AND BRIEF SPECIFICATION FOR THE ASTORIA

EXTERIOR OF THE ASTORIA, EASTER 1935 (Opening week). On the right hand of the photograph can be seen the end of the banner which stretched across the street advertising the opening film THE GAY DIVORCE. Note the current fashion for longer ladies' coats.

Occupying a prominent position in the centre of the town, the new cinema's frontage was imposing. The outstanding feature immediately above the entrance was a large open-air balcony, an extension of the first-floor café-restaurant, where 200 patrons could enjoy al fresco meals when the weather was fine. At night, the long glass channels recessed into the end towers on either side of the balcony were brightly illuminated, creating an oasis of light around the facade of the cinema. Access to the auditorium was through a large entrance hall with its centrally-sited paybox leading to the stalls foyer or, upstairs, to restaurant and circle foyer.

The auditorium was decorated in simple style with a rough-cast finish in shades of silver grey which, combined with a well-conceived scheme of indirect lighting, conveyed an atmosphere of warmth and comfort. An orchestra pit complete with Compton organ lay in front of the fully-equipped stage which was 36ft wide extending to 60ft beyond the tabs, with a depth of 20ft. The screen was set back 10ft from the footlights and during stage shows was raised electrically into the flies above. Stage lighting was controlled from a switchboard in the wings. Dressing rooms were provided. A safety curtain of steel weighing 6½ tons, a main rising curtain and a second pair of curtains completed the picture. Situated at the highest point of the building and separated from the auditorium by a wall of concrete 9" thick, was the projection room, with access to the open air on the roof. Two Ernemann projectors linked with Western Electric wide range sound apparatus, as well as a slide projector, were installed. The cinema was fully air-conditioned, air being introduced from the ceiling of the auditorium and foyers, with complete air-changes every ten minutes.

A capacity audience filled the 1666 seats in stalls and circle on the night of the Grand Opening, 20 April, 1935. The Board of Directors assembled on the stage to welcome the audience and there was a great sense of occasion. Jan Godowsky and his orchestra presented a lively programme of popular music commencing with 'Easter Parade' and Leslie Holman demonstrated the wonders of the £2,500 Compton organ. The film was *THE GAY DIVORCE* with Fred Astaire and Ginger Rogers, supported by a nature short, British Movietone News and the Gaumont British Magazine, perhaps justifiably billed overall as 'The Greatest Show in Folkestone's History'.

OPENING NIGHT: The Board of Directors of the locally-formed company assemble in the foyer of the theatre. Major C.H. Bell OBE, Managing Director and driving force behind the venture is on the extremem right.

Seat prices ranged from 9d in the front stalls to 2/6d in the Royal Circle. The reason why there were no seats at 6d or 7d was explained by the Managing Director: "We cannot afford to give away entertainment: we cannot produce entertainment of the type we intend to give, under 9d." But despite this statement, the following month saw the introduction of bargain matinée prices enabling patrons to enjoy a full 3-hour programme of films and live entertainment for as little as 6d.

In June 1936, the cinema changed hands, the new owners being the fast-growing County Cinemas Ltd. circuit, based in the southern counties. Business at the ASTORIA was very good and in June 1938 when the Cinematograph Exhibitors' Association (CEA for short) chose Folkestone for their summer conference, the ASTORIA was the chosen venue for two late-night trade shows. *ST MARTIN'S LANE*, starring Charles Laughton, was one of the films, with the star making a personal appearance; the other was *ALF'S BUTTON AFLOAT*, featuring the Crazy Gang. In fact, all the Folkestone cinemas put on special presentations for the 'Gala Week' of the conference, the week ending with a Film Star Ball at the Leas Cliff Hall. Before the Ball opened, such stars as Margaret Lockwood, Moore Marriott, Edgar Kennedy and Graham Moffat appeared in person at the ASTORIA, a proud moment for 'The Cinema Supreme'.

By the time war came in September, 1939, County Cinemas had merged with Oscar Deutsch's circuit, and in 1940 the familiar ODEON sign replaced ASTORIA as the theatre's name. During the war years, the ODEON made a full contribution to the war effort, providing entertainment and relaxation for members of the Armed Forces and the remaining civilians in the town. The Management also frequently placed the theatre at the disposal of organisers of various money-raising events such as War Weapons Week. And on one occasion the military took over the ODEON completely so that General Montgomery (Monty) could address the officers under his command.

THE GAY DIVORCE was a shrewd choice for the Grand Opening Gala of the ASTORIA on 20 April, 1935.

AUDITORIUM OF THE ASTORIA, GROUND FLOOR

THE ASTORIA'S COMPTON ORGAN in the UP position in the centre of the orchestra pit with the rising main curtain behind. The two organ chambers were sited, one above the other, behind the decorative grille to the right of the picture. The matching grille on the left hand side of the auditorium (not shown) masked an empty space. The 3 manual/6 rank organ, with lift, was first played by Leslie Holman in 1935. It is now in private hands in Holland.

REGINALD STONE on the stage of the ASTORIA with his Hammond Lafleur organ, February, 1939. Reedless and pipeless, it was one of the earliest electronic models so familiar today. Note: The screen has been "flown" and the stage curtains have been artistically draped to provide a suitable backdrop for the organist. Later the organ was transferred to the restaurant where dancing took place.

"ON STAGE" for the of THE ASTORIA. There are no less than 43 employees of the ASTORIA shown in this photograph, including restaurant staff. It shows the scale of employment in the cinema industry before the decline set in.

CHANGE OF NAME. The ASTORIA became the ODEON on 1st June, 1940, and this photograph of the staff line-up was taken next day.

In April 1956, the ODEON celebrated 21 years in the entertainment business and, on Monday 16 April, manager Mr Charles Smith marked the occasion by entertaining guests at a reception. A magnificent iced birthday cake depicting the facade of the cinema was presented to the Matron of the Royal Victoria Hospital who, with a party of uniformed nurses, was present at this 'coming of age'. Among the guests was Mr G.F. Ronco whose restaurant Maestrani's originally stood on the site of the ODEON. The anniversary programme appropriately featured a nursing drama, *THE FEMININE TOUCH*, and to round off the festivities a section of the restaurant was devoted to a Hobbies Exhibition with pride of place being given to a 1912 hand-cranked Pathé projector.

The remaining years of the ODEON's life makes sad reading, although the Rank Organisation did all they could to increase business. The interior of the cinema was renovated, re-styled and re-decorated; the projection room was automated; the restaurant became a disco, and there were one-night stands by pop stars. The Saturday morning children's film shows were well attended, these being the only occasions when the organ was fully employed and enjoyed. The management were also very successful in arranging personal appearances of such film stars as David Tomlinson, Jeremy Spenser and David Farrar.

THE ODEON occupied a prominent position in Folkestone's shopping area and, on demolition, Boots the Chemist were able to occupy a prime site. The photograph also shows the Town Hall (centre) which housed a CINEMA DE LUXE in the years just before World War I.

GALA PERFORMANCE of WEST SIDE STORY on 18 July 1962.

The last great occasion at the ODEON was a gala performance of *WEST SIDE STORY* on the evening of 18th July 1962 in aid of the Order of St. John, whose Appeal Committee Chairman, Diana Sheridan (Mrs John Davis) was introduced to the packed house. In addition to the outstanding film presentation, Norman Wisdom appeared on the stage, Gerald Shaw (from the ODEON, Leicester Square) played the organ and Harry Leader and his orchestra performed in the pit. It was a never-to-be-forgotten event for the cinema and the town.

A few more years were to pass before the curtain came down for the last time, but the end came suddenly for the ODEON. Local newspapers advertised a double-bill James Bond programme with *DIAMONDS ARE FOREVER* and *FROM RUSSIA WITH LOVE* for the week ending 26 January 1974 and there was no inkling of closure. But with only a small group of faithful filmgoers attending the final performance on that date, Folkestone's much-loved theatre passed quietly away. Soon the demolition contractors moved in, clearing the way for a new building to house Boots the Chemists.

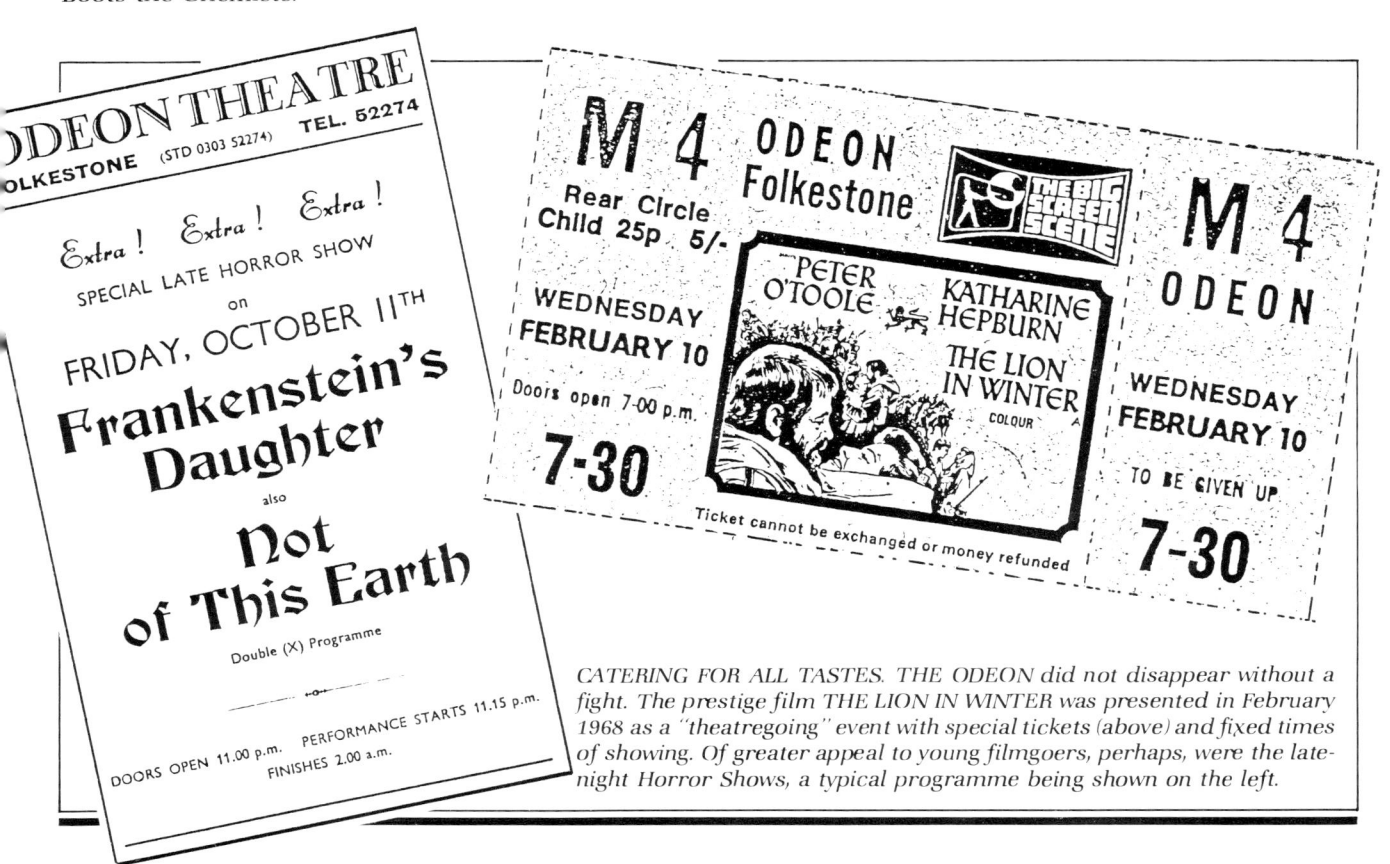

CATERING FOR ALL TASTES. THE ODEON did not disappear without a fight. The prestige film THE LION IN WINTER was presented in February 1968 as a "theatregoing" event with special tickets (above) and fixed times of showing. Of greater appeal to young filmgoers, perhaps, were the late-night Horror Shows, a typical programme being shown on the left.

When Charlie Chaplin visited Folkestone

"I was only a youngster in 1921 when Charlie Chaplin visited Folkestone, but I shall never forget the thrill of seeing the 'Little Fellow' in the flesh. And the fact that like me, he was born in London, made me feel very proud.

Chaplin had arrived for a European visit early in September 1921 on board the 'Olympic', one of his main objectives being to attend the premiere of his latest film *THE KID*, which introduced Jackie Coogan to the world. After the showing, Chaplin flew from Paris to Lympne on Wednesday, 28 September, where he was met and taken to Port Lympne, the residence of his host, Sir Philip Sassoon. The following afternoon, Sassoon took Chaplin to see the wounded ex-servicemen at the Star & Garter Home at Sandgate. The next day, Chaplin accompanied his host to the Wesleyan School, Grace Hill, Folkestone, where Sir Philip unveiled a war memorial to 29 former scholars who died in the first world war.

The crowds which milled around on this solemn occasion followed Chaplin and Sassoon as they left the school en route to the CENTRAL CINEMA in George Lane. There they were received by the Managing Director, George Thompson, who conducted them to the front row of the balcony. The lights were then lowered and a special screening of the film *NOT FORGOTTEN* took place. This short documentary included scenes of Sir Philip Sassoon entertaining the men of the Star and Garter Home. By now, the word had got around that Chaplin was in town and crowds surged round the cinema, waiting for the star. In the event, most of them were disappointed, but I was one of the lucky ones who spotted him and his host leaving by a side door, in the interests of safety. Next day I learned that Chaplin had left by road for London, and two weeks later I read that he was back in the USA making his next picture.

In later years I was to see in Folkestone such stars as Margaret Lockwood, Charles Laughton, Diana Wynyard, Michael Redgrave, Valerie Hobson, David Tomlinson and Phyllis Calvert coming to promote the local showings of their films. But none of them exuded the charm and personal aura of Charles Chaplin." *Mr K.P.*

FOOTNOTE. Most of the cinemas of Dover, Deal and Folkestone featured Chaplin films over the years, his most popular film being *THE GOLD RUSH* (1925), after which he spaced out his films to ensure public demand. Many of his films he wrote and directed, besides writing the music. Towards the end of his life he became Sir Charles Chaplin; he died in December 1977.

Thanks for the Memories

"At the ASTORIA I soon became known to the usherettes as the boy who always wanted the centre front seat, in order to get the best possible view of the organist performing. I would time my entry to catch the 3 pm interlude, which meant I also caught the 6 pm one at the end of the programme. It was not unknown for me to sit through the programme again just to enjoy the organ interlude once again.

My devotion was rewarded by the organist, who allowed me to attend a Sunday morning rehearsal for the coming week's interlude. This was always called the organist's solo but in reality was anything but a solo effort. The stage had to be draped and then bathed in a kaleidoscope of colours. This meant the projection staff were busy behind the scenes, especially when the organist required slides to be projected, telling the musical story or encouraging the audience to join in the sing-song. Imagine my schoolboy delight when I was left alone at the organ console to amuse myself while the men went off to the bar for refreshment. I went up and down the organ loft to the weird accompaniment of klaxon horns, steamboat whistles, bird songs, chimes and all the other effects and percussions incorporated in these lavish instruments.

So I began to teach myself to play the organ, practising in the empty cinema until finally I was allowed to 'play in' the patrons at the start of the show, and sometimes playing a few bars of music inbetween the trailers. All this took place with the organ console at the bottom of the lift, so that I was unseen. Then on the evening of Boxing Day 1945, I achieved my ambition: the manager agreed I could be given the full treatment, rising into sight of the packed audience and with a spotlight playing on me. What a thrill.

Service with the RAF during the war gave me few opportunities to play the organ, but after the war when I was working with a local firm, I managed to keep in practice. On a business trip to Dover, for example, I talked my way into the GRANADA and enjoyed the experience of playing their Christie organ. Then, in 1961, the SAVOY cinema switched to Bingo, and I eventually approached the manager to see if I might acquire the disused Standaart organ. He agreed and piece by piece, I transferred the organ to my house where, after some structural alterations I was able to install it. I still have this cinema organ in my home.

In 1968, when the ASTORIA had become the ODEON, it was announced that *WEST SIDE STORY* was to be given its provincial premiere there. Not only was the cinema given a face-lift but the organ was brought up to standard, ready for Gerald Shaw, renowned broadcasting organist from the ODEON, Leicester Square, to perform at the console. I enquired if I might record his performance, but was told this was forbidden. So with friends in high places I arranged to secrete myself beforehand in the void behind the left-hand auditorium grille, microphone at the ready through the grille.

The cinema that night was filled to capacity. Not only did I record Gerald Shaw's marvellous performance, but also Harry Leader and his orchestra plus the great Norman Wisdom himself; even though I couldn't see him performing, I had a good view of the audience who were killing themselves with laughter. That is how I will always remember the ASTORIA/ODEON, Folkestone's very special home of entertainment." **Eric Hart.**

"The ASTORIA was well-equipped for presenting organ solos as one could fly the screen and some fine stage settings with drapes and lighting enhanced the organ shows. I recall borrowing a church exterior stage set from the old PLEASURE GARDENS THEATRE when presenting 'In a Monastery Garden'. In that pre-war era we tried to make every show a 'Gala Performance'. I enjoyed every minute of it." **Reg Stone.** *(This well-known organist appeared at the ASTORIA Sept 1938/Nov 1939).*

ERIC HART with the Standaart organ he rescued from the SAVOY and installed in his home, thus saving the organ from destruction. It is 2 manual/7 rank with a fixed console and was introduced to SAVOY patrons in 1929, the organist being Percy Milton.

REG MOORE at the Crompton organ installed in the orchestra pit of the PLEASURE GARDENS THEATRE in 1949. The 2 manual/5 rank fixed console organ's original home was the REX/RENDEZVOUS cinema, Cambridge. When the PLEASURE GARDENS THEATRE was demolished in 1964, the organ perished with it, apart from some ranks of pipes and other souvenirs salvaged by a local organ enthusiast.

Thanks for the Memories

"It was in March 1935 that I saw a 'Situations Vacant' advertisement in the FOLKESTONE HERALD, for usherettes at the ASTORIA. Applicants were to apply personally at the Tontine Street Employment Exchange on 1st April. I was 18 then and duly presented myself for interview. Unfortunately I was only 5' 1" tall, instead of 5' 4", so the Astoria's manager, Billy Stewart, could only offer me a position as waitress in the cinema's restaurant. I accepted the job, but after three months another usherette vacancy arose and I was allowed to fill it, despite my lack of inches.

I discovered that it was not an easy job and the hours were long. We had to parade for daily inspection before the cinema opened and often remained on duty until the end of the last performance of the day. There were three 30-minute mealbreaks during the day: lunch, tea and supper, but otherwise I was on my feet the whole time. The main task was to show patrons to their seats, the other job being to sell ices and confectionery, which we took in turn. The rewards of the job consisted of one day off a week, one early evening (from 7pm), the provision of a uniform, an initial issue of court shoes and the princely sum of £1 a week.

During the war I moved to Bristol where I worked as an usherette at the ODEON. After a while, owing to projectionists being called up for H.M. Forces, I was trained as a projectionist. When I returned to Folkestone in 1945 I was engaged at the ASTORIA, now the ODEON, as a second projectionist, a job I thoroughly enjoyed. Later I was presented with an engraved, silver cigarette box by Mr A.J. Rockett, Operations Manager, Top Rank Theatres, for 25 years service with the cinema.

It was a sad day for me and all the staff when the ODEON was closed in 1974; it had been second home to us. Fortunately, the CENTRAL had just been tripled and I was engaged full-time. Later I left, for family reasons, but returned on a part-time basis, serving a total of 8½ happy years at that cinema." *Georgina May Johnson.*

PROJECTION ROOM of the ASTORIA, c.1935

PART FOUR

Folkestone in Wartime 1939-1945

Set against the background of World War II, this is an account of how Folkestone's cinemas fared, the films they showed and the supportive role they played during those difficult war years.

THE ODEON played its part in the preparations for the great campaign in North Africa (see 1942 section). The photograph above, reproduced by kind permission of the Imperial War Museum, shows Sir Bernard Montgomery, later Field-Marshal Viscount Montgomery of Alamein, observing operations from his tank at the Battle of Alamein.

1939

Sept 1: Germany invaded Poland. Sept 3: Great Britain and France declared war on Germany; B.E.F. began to leave for France.

THE STORY OF IRENE AND VERNON CASTLE

PROFESSOR MAMLOCK

CONFESSIONS OF A NAZI SPY

The first action of the government following the declaration of war on Sunday 3 September 1939 was to close all places of entertainment and, for a week, Folkestone's cinemas remained dark and deserted. At that time, the town boasted four cinema theatres - THE SAVOY, THE CENTRAL, THE PLAYHOUSE and THE ASTORIA. Monday 11 September saw the cinemas re-open, suitably blacked-out and with all outside lighting and neon signs switched off "for the duration". The general public were informed that special training had been given to staff and that in the event of an air-raid the house lights would be raised and an announcement would be made from the stage. The audience could either stay put - the performance would probably continue - or leave the theatre. However, in accordance with the government's ruling, all cinemas would close at 10 pm and no children would be admitted at any time without an adult.

In November 1939, Reginald Stone, who had been resident organist at the ASTORIA since September 1938, departed and was not replaced. He was next heard broadcasting from a camp "Somewhere in England".

THE LAMBETH WALK, and *THE STORY OF IRENE AND VERNON CASTLE* starring the Astaire/Rogers dance team were examples of the escapist fare screened during the first few months of the war but later came Warner Bros.' exposé of Nazi methods in the U.S.A., *CONFESSIONS OF A NAZI SPY; PROFESSOR MAMLOCK,* a Russian film made in 1938 about the persecution of a Jewish doctor in Germany; *THE SPY IN BLACK,* and *THE LION HAS WINGS,* a swiftly-assembled, all-star, flag-waving documentary patriotically produced by Alexander Korda. Distributed throughout the country at a nominal rental, *THE LION HAS WINGS* was screened at both the ASTORIA and SAVOY theatres. THE ASTORIA programme included Sonnie Hale in *LET'S BE FAMOUS,* a historic newsreel depicting scenes of yesteryear Folkestone and, at the console of the Crompton organ, Arthur Kingdon, a local musician who had deputised at the theatre from time to time.

'Friday night is Military Night' proclaimed the ASTORIA in December 1939: 'Army concerts and community singing in addition to films. 1,000 seats reserved for HMF in uniform at the reduced price of 1/-.' On these regular Friday night occasions, Arthur Kingdon was at the Crompton organ. On other nights, he could be found at the Leas Cliff Hall with his Hammond Lafleur electric organ - pipeless and reedless - where he played for dancing.

1940

Apr 9: Germany invaded Denmark and Norway. May 10: Germany invaded the Low Countries. June 22: France capitulated. Aug 3-Oct 31: German air offensive against Great Britain (Battle of Britain).

The Phoney War ended on 10 May when Germany invaded the Low Countries and France and, with the evacuation of the B.E.F. from Dunkirk, Folkestone found itself well and truly in the front line. But the show must go on, war or no war, and, despite all the difficulties, the town's cinemas continued to function, providing entertainment for all.

A large display advertisement in the 1 June issue of the Folkestone Herald announced 'You will see it at the Odeon - it was the Astoria' and the following day Arthur Kingdon played the ASTORIA out and the ODEON in before a crowded house.

The usherettes paraded in their smart new uniforms and visitors to the restaurant found that it had been completely refurbished with new tables, chairs and carpets whilst the windows had been splinterproofed. *CONTRABAND*, re-uniting the unlikely star team from *THE SPY IN BLACK*, Conrad Veidt and Valerie Hobson, was the opening attraction.

June 3 saw the evacuation of the B.E.F. completed. The day before, 3,200 schoolchildren left by special train for Wales. The first phase of what became known as the Battle of Britain took place on 10 July with attacks on shipping in the Channel and the air battles which continued right until the end of October.

Although, understandably, not reported in the local press at the time, there was an invasion alert one June evening when slides were superimposed over the pictures being screened at Folkestone's cinemas recalling all troops to barracks. It proved to be a false alarm but the troops stayed on the alert for many weeks.

On 27 July, the Folkestone Herald informed its readers that both the SAVOY and the PLAYHOUSE would be closing down after the last performance that day and that they might remain shut for the duration. "I suppose the plain truth is that there is not enough people in Folkestone to provide patrons for four cinemas", wrote the editor, and it is a fact that during the darkest days of the war the population went down from 50,000 to 9,000. The second phase of the Battle of Britain, attacks on Kentish airfields, commenced in August and on the 15th of that month a heavy raid, during which an enemy plane crashed into a power cable close to the electric light works, caused considerable problems in the town. Owing to lack of power, performances at the town's two remaining cinemas, the ODEON and CENTRAL, were cancelled; ironically only a short while before, the CENTRAL had changed over from its own independent supply to that of the town. By now, the ODEON and CENTRAL were working closely together, advertising in a joint display block in the local press as well as promoting each other's programmes by means of slides and posters. They were also sharing the same Movietone newsreel. As there was a shortage of film stock, it had been decreed that cinemas showing the same newsreel would share one copy with the result that junior staff were forever rushing from one theatre to another clutching the precious can of film. The ruling was that it was the responsibility of the cinema next showing the news to collect the reel from the other hall and, whilst in the main this arrangement worked well, there were hair-raising moments when exhibition times virtually clashed.

The Folkestone Herald Spitfire Fund - with a target of £5,000 - was inaugurated in August. The ODEON staged an exhibition in the foyer of trophies of Nazi planes shot down in Kent and followed this up with a Sunday concert which benefitted the fund by around £100.

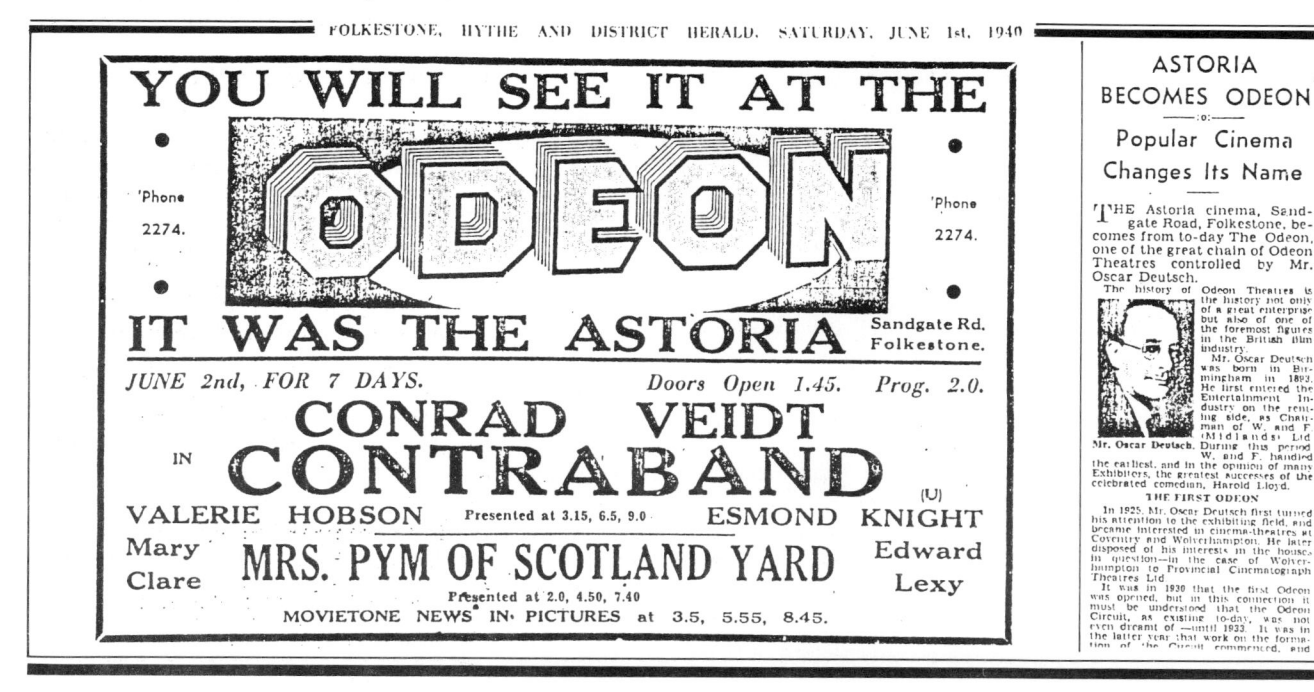

FOLKESTONE, HYTHE AND DISTRICT HERALD, SATURDAY, JUNE 1st, 1940

YOU WILL SEE IT AT THE ODEON

'Phone 2274.

IT WAS THE ASTORIA — Sandgate Rd. Folkestone.

JUNE 2nd, FOR 7 DAYS.   Doors Open 1.45.   Prog. 2.0.

CONRAD VEIDT
in
CONTRABAND (U)

VALERIE HOBSON   Presented at 3.15, 6.5, 9.0   ESMOND KNIGHT

Mary Clare   **MRS. PYM OF SCOTLAND YARD**   Edward Lexy

Presented at 2.0, 4.50, 7.40

MOVIETONE NEWS IN PICTURES at 3.5, 5.55, 8.45.

ASTORIA BECOMES ODEON

Popular Cinema Changes Its Name

THE Astoria cinema, Sandgate Road, Folkestone, becomes from to-day The Odeon, one of the great chain of Odeon Theatres controlled by Mr. Oscar Deutsch.

The history of Odeon Theatres is the history not only of a great enterprise but also of one of the foremost figures in the British film industry.

Mr. Oscar Deutsch was born in Birmingham in 1893. He first entered the Entertainment Industry on the renting side, as Chairman of W. and F. (Midlands) Ltd. During this period W. and F. handled the earliest, and in the opinion of many Exhibitors, the greatest successes of the celebrated comedian, Harold Lloyd.

THE FIRST ODEON

In 1925, Mr. Oscar Deutsch first turned his attention to the exhibiting field, and became interested in cinema-theatres at Coventry and Wolverhampton. He later disposed of his interests in the houses in question—in the case of Wolverhampton to Provincial Cinematograph Theatres Ltd.

It was in 1930 that the first Odeon was opened, but in this connection it must be understood that the Odeon Circuit, as existing to-day, was not even dreamt of —until 1933. It was in the latter year that work on the formation of the Circuit commenced, and

110

1941

Apr 6: Germany invaded Greece. Apr 12-Dec 9: Siege of Tobruk. June 22: Germany invaded Russia. Dec 7: Japanese attack Pearl Harbor. Dec 8: Great Britain and U.S.A. declared war on Japan.

THE GREAT DICTATOR

TARGET FOR TONIGHT

KIPPS

Chaplin's satire *THE GREAT DICTATOR* was screened at the ODEON in January 1941 and the Mayor and Mayoress were among the guests invited to see this picture. From comments in the local press, it was received with mixed feelings. The following month, the Ministry of Information (MOI) took over the ODEON on a Saturady morning and presented a special show of short films - "Documentary evidence of Britain's Victory Drive.... the answer to the question 'Am I taking my part?' ". Arthur Kingdon and Roma supplied the music as on many other wartime occasions. War Weapons Week was inaugurated from the stage of the ODEON on 5 May and a gala performance attended by the Mayor and his wife added to the festivities.

Basil Fortesque, who was managing director of Folkestone Amalgamated Cinemas during the Thirties, had by now joined Harry Bentley as general and booking manager of the circuit and it was no doubt due to his influence that the CENTRAL secured the premiere presentation of H.G. Wells' much-loved *KIPPS*. The CENTRAL naturally made the most of the occasion and took a large display advertisement on the front page of the Folkestone Herald - 'World Premiere - Special gala opening - Will not be seen again for weeks - Personal appearance of the stars.'

The great event took place on Monday 12 May at 7 pm. A flower-bedecked platform had been set up in front of the proscenium arch, and after the performance, the Mayor, Alderman G.A. Gurr, introduced the stars - Diana Wynyard (who made a short speech), Phyllis Calvert and Michael Redgrave - to the bedazzled audience. Later the stars went on to the Leas Cliff Hall where a Film Star Ball in their honour was being held and where they received an enthusiastic reception. The day ended with an informal supper at the Queens Hotel. Each and every event was recorded by the Movietone News cameraman as part of the publicity drive to promote the film in the U.S.A. The party that had travelled down from London for this memorable occasion included Carol Reed and Edward Black, respectively director and producer of *KIPPS*; Francis L. Hartley, managing director of 20th Century-Fox in this country; and Maurice Ostrer, who was in charge of production at the Gaumont-British studios at Shepherd's Bush. In addition, there were critics from British and American papers, all of whom had been granted special permission by the Chief Constable to enter a Defence Area.

The following day, Tuesday 13 May, the Mayor and Mayoress, along with other guests, attended the re-opening of the SAVOY, closed since July 1940.

Whilst the ASTORIA and REGAL cinemas at Margate were completely destroyed during the early days of the war, Folkestone's ODEON bore a charmed life. The only recorded incident took place on 16 May 1941 when twelve Me 109's machine-gunned the town, skimming low over the rooftops, and a stray bullet pierced the roof, injuring a soldier in the theatre. In July, the local paper reported that the CENTRAL was employing girls as cinema operators. A photograph showed Miss A. Ford (21) and Miss M. Bowbrick (19), both former usherettes, grappling with the projector.

The RAF documentary *TARGET FOR TONIGHT* was screened the same week of September at all three cinemas (there may well have been only one print which was rushed from theatre to theatre!) but ODEON manager W.R. Wright distinguished himself by arranging a special stage prologue featuring A.T.C. cadets and inviting the Mayor and Mayoress as honoured guests.

CENTRAL manager Andrew Drennan was in the limelight the following month when, on behalf of 20th Century Fox, he presented to the Mayor a copy of the Movietone newsreel made on the occasion of the premiere of *KIPPS* to be deposited at the town's archives. The general public was later able to see this newsreel, along with a selection of MOI short films, at a Saturday morning performance held at the ODEON in November as part of a propaganda drive by the MOI. Perhaps more to the liking of the entertainment-hungry public was a programme screened at the ODEON for a week in November and promoted as '*6 HAPPY DAYS WITH DEANNA*' : six films featuring the young Canadian singing star Deanna Durbin were shown during the week, a different picture each day.

1942

Feb 15: Fall of Singapore. Oct 23-Nov 4: German-Italian army defeated at El Alamein. Nov 8: British and American forces land in North Africa.

THE FIRST OF THE FEW

NEXT OF KIN

MRS MINIVER

The CENTRAL and ODEON were still sharing a display advertisement in the local press in January 1942 with the ODEON additionally publicising its restaurant and bar and promising dancing each evening.

Folkestone's Warship Week took place in March and the ODEON played a leading part by arranging a dance and also a variety show featuring Arthur Kingdon and talent from the Forces. The same month at London's Leicester Square Odeon, the sum of £60,000, collected from audiences at Odeon theatres throughout the country, was handed over to be divided between the Red Cross and Comforts Funds of the Navy, Army and Air Force. It is recorded that £205 had been donated by patrons of the ODEON Folkestone who also gave the following month the sum of £110 after seeing a short film depicting the work of the R.A.F. Benevolent Fund.

There was one wartime occasion when the ODEON was taken over by the Military but this did not come to light until some years later. In April 1956, the theatre celebrated the 21st anniversary of its opening and the editor of the Folkestone Herald, masquerading as 'The Roamer', recalled the events of past years and disclosed what happened when Monty made a personal appearance on the stage of the ODEON:

"I remember.... The morning when you could not get, so to speak, within a mile of the ODEON. Everywhere round the building Military Police patrolled, at every door Redcaps stood guard, not even the staff were allowed to pass into the cinema. Inside Sir Bernard Montgomery, later Field Marshal Viscount Montgomery, stood on the platform addressing an audience of officers of the Eastern Command. What did he tell them?! His plans for the training of troops for the great campaign in North Africa".

Harold Ramsay, the well-known broadcasting organist and one-time Controller of Entertainment for Union Cinemas, paid the town a visit in July, appearing at the ENSA-controlled PLEASURE GARDENS THEATRE where he entertained members of H.M. Forces with his Hammond electronic organ. On Saturday 15 August, during an air-raid, a bomb fell at the back of Church Street hitting an air-raid shelter. The CENTRAL, no more than twenty-five yards away from the seat of the explosion, was shaken but there was no panic in the theatre although a few people left after the incident and, eventually, the performance was resumed. A bus curfew was imposed in December with the result that buses ceased to operate after 9pm, a blow to cinemagoers living outside the town's limits.

Of the many films screened during 1942, three were of especial interest - *NEXT OF KIN*, an entertaining instructional film made for the Services which achieved commercial success; *THE FIRST OF THE FEW* starring Leslie Howard as R.J. Mitchell of Spitfire fame; and MGM's *MRS MINIVER*, the picture that was said to have played a leading part in influencing American opinion. Last, but not least, mention must be made of MOI short *21 MILES* (with commentary by Ed Murrow of CBS) which dealt with the ports bordering the English Channel in their wartime roles.

1943

May 13: Axis forces in Tunisia surrendered. June 10: Allies invaded Sicily. Sept 3: Allies invaded Italy. Sept 8: Italy capitulated.

IN WHICH WE SERVE

THE GENTLE SEX

Kinematograph Weekly, following a visit to the Kent coast by their special representative, published a four-page article dramatically headlined 'Exhibitors under fire' and going on to explain that 'This is the story of how, for three years, the Exhibitors of Dover, Deal, Folkestone and Hythe have kept the show going in the face of great dangers. They have been bombed, dive-bombed, machine-gunned and shelled but they have played an exemplary part in maintaining the highest traditions of showmanship at Hellfire Corner, England, S.E..'

Writing of Folkestone, Kinematograph Weekly described visiting the town's three theatres:

> 'Let me deal with the CENTRAL first. It lies down the hill back in the middle of an arcade and has two approaches from the street. Once upon a time it was a Walter Bentley property but now it has been taken over by Elcock's Mayfair Circuit. Perhaps the Mayfair directors will do something about the hall and give it even a modicum of renovation and cleaning because three years of front-line conditions and bombs and shells falling so near it have not improved the interior from the point of wallpaper. An old-fashioned house, it has a balcony as well as a circle. The balcony has one of the sharpest ramps I have seen but its serves its purpose for the underpaid British Tommy because he can have tenpennyworth up in 'the Gods'.
>
> Not fifty yards away further down the hill is the SAVOY, controlled by London and Provincial Cinemas. The manager is A.H. Hill who also runs the GROVE kinema, Hythe.... He is particularly keen on his cafe, quite small, but it's mainly devoted to giving troops a good meal as well as a good show....
>
> The third hall is the inevitable ODEON. A magnificent 1,660-seater with imposing foyer, fine restaurant and cafe, dance floor, bar and a stage. This ODEON is run with a slick efficiency that is hard to beat. It is unobtrusive and yet the whole building reeks of first-class showmanship. What a joy to see a man, only twenty-five miles from the enemy-occupied territory, well turned out in white tie and tails - not just another dress suit. The wearer is manager L.A. Stammers.'

Wings for Victory Week, yet another fund-raising campaign, took place in May. Lt Gen Sir William Dobbie was the principal speaker on Saturday 29 May at the ODEON, and was ably backed by the Mayor and Mayoress and by Rupert Brabner MP. An exhibition of photographs of blitzed German planes was mounted in the ODEON lobby.

Two tragic events took place in 1943 - in June, a CENTRAL usherette was found murdered, and in November a cooling fan at the SAVOY fell into the auditorium, killing a boy and injuring his companion. Among the films shown in 1943 there were two of especial wartime interest - Noel Coward's *IN WHICH WE SERVE*, a tribute to the Navy, and *THE GENTLE SEX*, which depicted life in the A.T.S. Two well-known theatre organists - Richard Foort and Reginald New - paid flying visits to Folkestone during the year appearing not at a local cinema but at the Forces Forum held at the Radnor Park Congregational Church.

1944

June 4: Rome captured. June 6: Allies landed in Normandy. June 13: Flying bomb (VI) attack on Britain started. Aug 25: Paris liberated. Sept 3: Brussels liberated.

GONE WITH THE WIND

The invasion of Europe by the Allies took place on 6 June and Folkestone breathed again, although not for long. Soon the skies were filled with pilotless aircraft, the V-1 or doodlebug as it was nicknamed, and the town found itself very much in the front line once more. On one occasion that fateful month, standing in the outside doorway of the CENTRAL's projection room, four of the operating team witnessed at first hand the death of a flying bomb at the hands of two Tempest fighters. 13 June saw the heaviest cross-Channel shelling that Folkestone had seen, some five hours in all. It was probably on this occasion that the CENTRAL was grazed by a passing shell. Whilst air-raid warnings were largely ignored by filmgoers intent on seeing their favourite stars, when the shell warning sounded (a double air-raid warning), all places of entertainment had to be cleared and performances were not recommenced until the "all-clear" had sounded.

July saw the evacuation of the 900-strong audience from the CENTRAL during the showing of *SPOTLIGHT SCANDALS*. Len Petts, junior projectionist at the CENTRAL at the time, has vivid memories of the occasion.

> 'It happened one evening as we were about to start the feature. Film caught alight on the re-wind bench and before we knew where we were the whole re-wind room was alight. The metal clad fire door saved the projection room and one reel of film. I estimate that 60,000ft of film went up in that blaze and when anybody hints to me even now on the futility of fire regulations, I quickly put them right. The CENTRAL was saved that night because the regulations were observed. We were, however, closed for a fortnight.'

At the end of August, Folkestone was opened to visitors despite the fact that the long-range guns across the Channel were still operating. One of the town's attractions was the screening of the MGM blockbuster *GONE WITH THE WIND* at the CENTRAL. It was a case of 'better late than never' for Dover filmgoers had had the opportunity of seeing this epic two years previously. The last shells fell on the town on 25 September 1944 and in October the King and Queen paid the battered port a visit.

1945

May 3: German forces in Italy surrendered. May 5: all German forces in Holland, NW Germany and Denmark surrendered unconditionally. Aug 4: Japan surrendered.

WESTERN APPROACHES

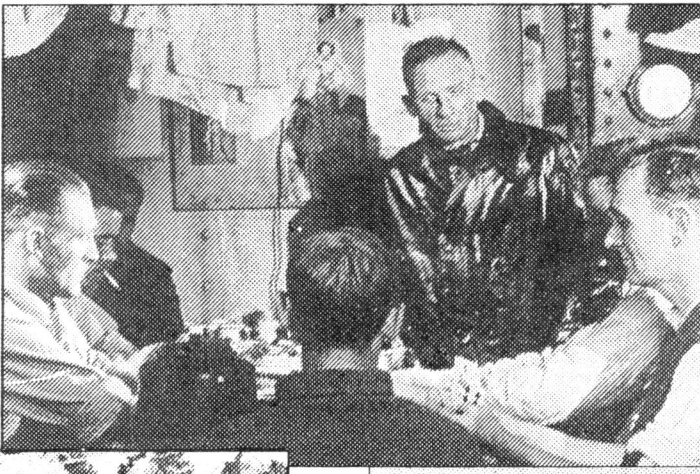

THE TRUE GLORY

GULLIVER'S TRAVELS

Escapist films continued to provide the staple fare for the cinemas in the year to come but from time to time films about the war intruded - WESTERN APPROACHES, 30 SECONDS OVER TOKYO, THE WAY TO THE STARS and THE TRUE GLORY were all shown in 1945. They were, naturally, overshadowed by the course of the war and the eventual surrender of Germany in May and Japan in August.

August 25 saw the Mayor re-opening the ODEON Cinema Club for Boys and Girls, the full-length cartoon film GULLIVER'S TRAVELS being the opening attraction. The ODEON was again in the news the following month when Thanksgiving Week - with a target of £175,000 - made its debut at the theatre. The Borough Member, H.R. Mackeson, aided by local dignitaries and the Band of the Royal Marines, Deal, were all present on Saturday 22 September and their efforts resulted in the sum of over £200,000 being raised.

The PLAYHOUSE did not re-open until 1 April 1946 following extensive refurbishment - new seating, heating and ventilation systems plus new projectors and the latest Western Electric Mirrophonic Sound System. The theatre had suffered some war damage but, despite a shortage of materials, this was soon put in hand. Both the CENTRAL and the PLAYHOUSE were now part of the fast-expanding, Newcastle-based Essoldo Circuit and Sol Sheckman, governing director of Essoldo, travelled to Folkestone to attend the gala re-opening, the main attraction being SCARLET STREET starring Edward G. Robinson. At the time, it was hinted that Essoldo intended building a brand-new super-cinema in the town but nothing ever came of it. Organ-lovers were highly delighted when Handel Evans took up residence at the ODEON in February and later on in the summer Arthur Kingdon was welcomed back at the Leas Cliff Hall with his 'Theatre Organ plus'. Victory Day was celebrated in Folkestone on 8 June 1946 but the excited crowds that thronged the streets were not to know that before life could return to normal, many dark and difficult days would have to be patiently endured. Dark and difficult years lay ahead for the Film Industry, too, and it is interesting to speculate whether John Jarrett, when addressing a conference for ODEON managers held at Folkestone in November 1946, had an inkling of the magnitude of the problems with which they would be confronted in the post-war period.

Acknowledgements

The authors gratefully acknowledge the co-operation and help received from the following:

Newspapers: Adscene, Dover Express, East Kent Mercury, Extra, Folkestone Herald, People and Kent Messenger (permission to reproduce photographs and for publicity).

KCC Libraries: Dover, Deal and Folkestone branches (research facilities).

British Film Institute: Information and Publications Departments; National Film Archive (photographs).

Local Historians: John Gilham, Ivan Green, Joe Harden and Bob Hollingsbee (Dover); Alan Taylor (Folkestone); Les Couzens, Julie Deller and John Turner (Deal). (Loan or gift of photographs).

Correspondents: It is impossible to list the names of all the kind people who wrote to, or telephoned, the authors, but the following loaned or gifted photographs and memoribilia: Mrs V. Arrindell, Lord Bernstein, Mrs J. Blair, Mr E. Blanche, Mr P. Collard, Mrs Cooper, Mrs S. Dunford, Miss J. Gladwell, Mrs Gumbrill, Mr E. Hart, Mrs J. Healey, Mrs P. Hewlett, Miss G. Johnson, Mrs J. Marsh, Mr W. Moore, Mr J. Morecroft, Mrs D. Neame, Mrs N. Osborne, Mrs B. Phasey, Mr L. Petts, Mr D. Pout, Mr Robinson, Royal Marines (Deal), Royal Marines Museum (Eastney), Mrs U. Savage and Mrs M. Tweedie.

Mr Ray Warner: His re-processing of old photographs and slides sent to the authors has been invaluable.

Wiggins Teape (UK) plc: Donation of paper for the book.

General: Acknowledgements as shown in text and also to Premier Bioscope and John D. Sharp (cinema photographs).

Mr Bob Adams and the staff of A.R. Adams & Sons (Printers) Ltd: Without their dedicated work this book would never have been produced so superbly and on time.

Special Note

Although every effort has been made to trace the present copyright holders of material used, the authors apologise for any unintentional omission or neglect and will be glad to insert the appropriate acknowledgements to companies or individuals in any subsequent edition of this book. The same applies in respect of any errors in factual material: additional or corrected information would be warmly welcomed.

The Cinema Theatre Association

If you have enjoyed reading this book and would like to enlarge your knowledge about cinemas, theatres and other entertainment buildings, the authors recommend membership of the Cinema Theatre Association. All aspects of cinemas and theatres are studied and wherever possible the Association campaigns for the preservation and continued use of such buildings for their original purpose. Visits, lectures, talks and film shows are arranged. For the modest membership fee, the Association also provides two publications: PICTURE HOUSE and CTA BULLETIN. Full details can be obtained from the Membership Secretary: Mr W. Wren, 53 Wenham Drive, Westcliffe-on-Sea, Essex, SS0 9BJ.